A Cultural History
of the
United States

■

Through the Decades

The 1910s

Michael V. Uschan

Lucent Books, Inc., San Diego, California

To Evie Kelvie, a second mom.

Library of Congress Cataloging-in-Publication Data

Uschan, Michael V., 1948–
    The 1910s / by Michael V. Uschan
       p.   cm.—(A cultural history of the United States through
the decades)
    Includes bibliographical references (p.   ) and index.
    Summary: Describes aspects of the political, economic, and
cultural life of the United States between 1910 and 1919 including
the Progressive Movement, World War I, and the silent film.
    ISBN 1-56006-551-6 (lib.bdg.: alk. paper)
    1. United States—History—1909–1913 —Juvenile literature.
2. United States—History—1913–1921 —Juvenile literature.
3. Nineteen tens—Juvenile literature. [1. United States—History—
1909–1913. 2. United States—History—1913–1921. 3. Nineteen tens.]
I. Title. II. Series.
E761.U83   1999
973.91—dc21
                                               98-24574
                                                 CIP
                                                     AC

Contents

Introduction: A Time of Change 4

Chapter One: The Progressive Movement and
    Woodrow Wilson 8

Chapter Two: The Fight for Rights 21

Chapter Three: Popular Culture: Silent Films,
    Vaudeville, and the Model T 36

Chapter Four: Edging into World Affairs 50

Chapter Five: The United States Goes to War 60

Chapter Six: The United States Helps Win the War 79

Chapter Seven: The Postwar Period 92

Epilogue: A Mood of Pessimism 106

Notes 110

Chronology 114

For Further Reading 120

Works Consulted 121

Index 123

Picture Credits 128

About the Author 128

The tenement district in New York City (Orchard Street as viewed from East Houston Street) is typical of the cramped, crowded, debris-strewn big city slums in which millions of poor Americans lived at the turn of the century. Housing was primitive and often substandard, but it was all many people could afford.

A Time of Change

As the twentieth century dawned, life in the United States was very different than it had been just a few decades earlier. Fueled by a massive wave of immigration in 1900, the nation's population of 76 million was nearly double that of just three decades earlier. One in seven residents had been born in a foreign country. Great changes had also taken place in the jobs Americans held and where they lived.

In 1860 fully 60 percent of Americans had worked in agriculture; by 1900 only 35 percent still labored on farms and ranches. Millions of workers now toiled in the plants, factories, and mills that were part of the Industrial Revolution.

Urban areas had grown explosively as immigrants and rural Americans crowded there in search of jobs. Although in 1870 four out of every five Americans lived in small rural communities, by 1900 nearly 40 percent resided in cities and towns with populations of eight thousand or more.

Americans were struggling to deal with these dramatic changes as well as new twentieth-century problems that stemmed from three major factors: immigration, urbanization, and industrialization.

The Industrial Revolution

By 1900 the United States had become the world's richest industrial nation, producing 31.9 percent of the coal, 36.7 percent of the steel, and 34.1 percent of the iron the world consumed as well as thousands of other products. But the way the Industrial Revolution had transformed the nation's economy since the end of the Civil War had created a new, troublesome social order.

The tremendous profits generated by this economic success were controlled by a relatively small number of people who owned the nation's factories, railroads, meatpacking plants, textile mills, and banks. And in the final decades of the nineteenth century industrialists and bankers had dramatically increased their power by consolidating into trusts, giant business combinations that could dominate entire segments of the economy.

The result was that in 1900 just 1 percent of Americans held more than half the nation's wealth; 12 percent owned nearly nine-tenths of it. With this wealth came political power that made those business-

men the new ruling class in America.

But as the power of big business grew, workers became weaker. The Industrial Revolution had replaced skilled workers, artisans, and craftsmen with machines that mass-produced everything from clothes to horse-drawn buggies, which were still more popular than the automobile. These unskilled workers, powerless to effectively challenge the companies that hired them, became part of a new lower class that lived in poverty.

Farmers were also nearly powerless in dealing with big business, which controlled both the markets that bought farm products and the railroads that transported them. Farmers of this era were also becoming dependent on banks for loans to buy new and increasingly necessary machinery such as harvesters.

Even in the century's second decade one-third to one-half of the working population labored twelve hours a day at brutally hard, often dangerous jobs. One steelworker commented that "home is just the place where I eat and sleep. I live in the mills."[1] Most earned little more than a dollar a day, a wage barely enough to allow them to survive. These workers included an estimated 1.5 million boys and girls under thirteen, which meant a child in 1900 was as likely to be laboring in a mine or factory as attending school.

In his 1904 book *Poverty*, Robert Hunter estimated that at the turn of the

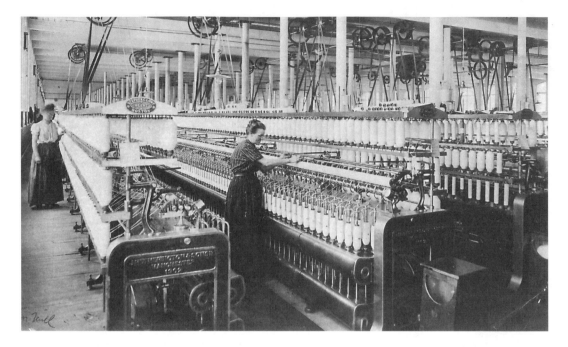

A worker in a cotton mill, circa 1910, tends one of the machines that helped the Industrial Revolution reshape the nation's economy. Machines had now become more important than people in producing goods.

century 10 million of America's 76 million citizens lacked "a sanitary dwelling and sufficient food and clothing to keep the body in working order." Hunter concluded that this standard of living "was below [what] a man would demand for his horses."[2.]

Problems in Big Cities

Immigrants and rural Americans had crowded into the nation's big cities because, as the centers of industry, finding jobs was more likely there. The result was that at the turn of the century poverty-stricken workers accounted for at least half

the population in cities like New York and Chicago.

More than a million immigrants arrived in the United States each year until 1914, a significant demographic change. The first immigrants to this country had almost always headed west to the frontier, where they could acquire a homestead of 160 acres from the government for free and build a life for themselves. But the frontier had vanished by 1890, and recent immigrants settled instead in the cities, where their inability to speak English and lack of education doomed them to menial jobs. Many never escaped the poverty they found in their new homeland, although their better-educated children generally did.

Cities staggered under their tremendous growth, which had strained financial and social resources. Between 1860 and 1900 New York City grew from 1 million to 3.5 million, Philadelphia from 500,000 to 1.3 million, Boston from 170,000 to more than 500,000, and Chicago from a small city to almost 1.7 million. The number of cities with more than 100,000 residents increased from 9 to 50.

All too often, city governments in this era were run by corrupt political organizations that did nothing to stop the spread of poverty and slums. The working poor were jammed into foul-smelling, run-down tenement buildings in which entire families lived in single rooms that lacked windows for ventilation. Families on each floor used a communal washbasin and shared a privy, a primitive toilet located in the basement.

The Progressive Movement

But as the twentieth century opened these and other problems began to generate a wave of reform. Two presidents—Republican Theodore Roosevelt and Democrat Woodrow Wilson—would lead this fight.

A mother and daughter, their faces showing the strain of their long trip and perhaps a hint of fear for the future, sit on a bench while awaiting processing along with other newly arrived immigrants.

Their goal was simple: to revitalize the American Dream. From the time of the Pilgrims people from around the world had been lured to America by a single, wonderful promise—if they worked hard they could make a good life for themselves.

In the twentieth century this dream was dying for millions of people. The Progressives wanted to make it live once again.

Chapter One

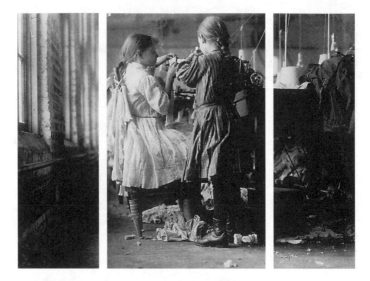

In 1910 two young girls work as a raveler and looper at the Loudon, Tennessee, Hosiery Mills. Millions of poor children who should have been in school were forced to labor in factories, mines, and other industries to help support their families.

The Progressive Movement and Woodrow Wilson

The Progressive movement was a wide-ranging, turn-of-the-century reform effort by Americans from all walks of life who held a wide variety of beliefs, pursued many different goals, and belonged to many political parties. They included farmers, unskilled workers, labor unions, radical groups like the Socialists, and minor political movements that worked for specific goals such as women's suffrage and Prohibition.

The heart of the movement, however, was the middle class, whose members were filled with compassion and anger over the era's human misery. They were outraged by rising levels of crime, overcrowding, and substandard living conditions for the poor in big cities; children as young as eight working long hours in textile mills and coal mines; and corrupt government officials.

Their overriding concern was an economic system, dominated by big business, that virtually enslaved millions of workers. In the second decade of the twentieth century from one-third to one-half of workers labored up to twelve hours a day, sometimes seven days a week, for bare subsistence wages.

The middle class—professionals and educated people such as doctors, lawyers, teachers, ministers, and small businessmen—was also worried about its own future. Its members had seen their standing in society erode as the wealthy became more powerful. They were worried about the ultimate narrowing of their own opportunities to better themselves economically and socially. So their compassion for others was linked with concern for their own future.

Progressives fought to give citizens more political power and clean up government corruption, help the poor, and, above all, limit the size and power of big business. They tried to help workers by supporting proposals for reduced working hours, workplace safety, limits on child labor, safeguards for women workers, old age pensions, and workers' compensation for people injured on the job.

Big Business and Trusts

A basic belief of the Progressive movement was that the growing economic and political dominance of big business was the cause of most of society's ills. In the late 1890s and early years of the new century many businesses had consolidated into giant trusts, which overpowered competition and controlled segments of industry such as steel, meatpacking, oil, sugar, tobacco, farm equipment, and mining. Because trusts were virtual monopolies and

John D. Rockefeller, one of the turn of the century's richest, most powerful business leaders. The immense wealth Rockefeller amassed and his rich lifestyle contrasted sharply to the harsh poverty in which millions of Americans lived.

no government regulation was in effect, trusts could set their own prices and operate as they wished.

John D. Rockefeller, whose Standard Oil Company at one time produced 97 percent of the nation's oil, defended trusts as a way for businessmen to "work together for the economies [it gave them] and enjoy the success." But most Americans felt such entities existed to make businessmen fabulously wealthy at their own expense. Meatpacking giant Philip D. Armour confirmed the nation's greedy view of businessmen when he admitted, "I do love the getting of it [money]."[3]

Among the most powerful trusts were railroads, the era's only national form of mass transportation. Because all commercial goods were shipped by rail, from cattle and grain to steel beams and clothing, railroads wielded immense economic power. They set their own rates and offered lower prices, called rebates, and other economic advantages to preferred customers, further eliminating competition and leading to greater business consolidation.

Because forming a trust involved considerable costs, banks and other financial firms wielded more power than ever. In the early years of the twentieth century, J. Pierpont Morgan was the nation's richest, most influential banker. In 1895, when the United States needed an emergency loan of $65 million in gold, President Grover Cleveland borrowed it from Morgan.

It was also Morgan who in 1901 created the United States Steel Corporation by buying eight steel companies and a host of subsidiary firms. This trust was the largest company the world had ever seen, the first to be incorporated at more than $1 billion.

The growing power of Morgan and other powerful bankers who operated mainly out of New York consolidated the nation's financial power in one area. This hurt farmers and businesses in other areas of the nation because it limited their access to the capital they needed.

The concentration of wealth in big business enabled industrialists and financiers to exert undue control over political parties and elected officials; the result was legislation that favored business interests over average people. Big business, for example, backed high tariffs—duties placed on imported products—because they reduced competition and allowed U.S. firms to charge higher prices. Businesses also corrupted many public officials by bribing them to secure government contracts or special privileges.

Progressive Philosophy

Progressives believed that people by nature were decent and well intentioned and that the structure of the nation's economy and government was responsible for the era's poverty and misery. This philosophy departed from the beliefs of many Americans, who claimed people were poor because

Child Labor

By 1910 one out of every five children under the age of fifteen was employed. Children as young as five or six tended huge rows of machines in textile mills, descended into the darkness of coal mines, and toiled in garment-district sweatshops.

Child labor was perhaps the ugliest new reality of the Industrial Revolution, the one that horrified Progressives like no other. The number of child workers kept growing because of two factors: (1) manufacturers paid children less and (2) children needed to work so their families could survive.

"When I was twelve years old my mother said I had to leave school and get a job," a Philadelphia man quoted in *The Twentieth Century* who worked as a child said years later, "We needed the money, so I got a job makin' button holes in vests. Start at seven, work till six, six days a week. I got three cents for every two button holes, and I made them by hand. Oh, you had to make an awful lot. The first week I made 265 and they gave me four dollars."

When journalist George Creel investigated child labor In 1913 he found children working in coal mines, sweatshops, cotton mills, shrimp canneries, factories, and other industries. In *America Enters the World,* Creel estimated 2 million children were "being fed annually into the steel hoppers of the modern industrial machine" each year and emerging "mangled in mind, body, and soul, and aborted into a maturity robbed of power and promise."

Thousands were injured on the job, especially in textile mills where they tended

A small child labors in a New York garment factory. His dirty face and the haunting look in his eyes mirror the difficult life he and other youngsters were forced to lead to earn enough money to survive.

machines with whirling blades that cut cloth. In a 1903 strike at a textile mill in Kensington, Pennsylvania, ten thousand of the seventy-five thousand workers were small children. This is how Mary "Mother" Jones, a union activist, described the young workers in *America Enters the World:* "Every day little children came into Union Headquarters, some with their hands off, some with the thumb missing, some with their fingers off at the knuckle. They were stooped little things, round shouldered and skinny. Many were not over ten years of age."

The greatest tragedy was they could not go to school, dooming them to a lifetime of unskilled labor and poverty.

they were lazy or had other character defects that caused them to fail.

Although Progressives rejected arguments by Socialists, Communists, and other radicals that capitalism was evil and must be overthrown, they realized major changes were needed to solve the country's new problems. The result was that Progressives adopted two underlying beliefs that broke with the past and set the stage for reform.

The first idea was to reject laissez-faire, an economic theory that advocated minimal government control over private enterprise. Progressives believed business interests had grown so powerful that they had to be curbed in the interest of all Americans. The second was that government itself must be the driving force behind economic and social change to remedy modern problems. In the past government officials had limited themselves to providing basic services and refrained from trying to effect social change. But government, especially the federal government, now seemed the only agent powerful enough to turn to for reform.

These two shifts in philosophy cleared the way for the rise of activist politicians. But before this could happen the public had to become aware of the problems the Progressives sought to solve.

One of the movement's most important allies in the century's first decade was a group of writers dubbed muckrakers. President Theodore Roosevelt gave them this name by comparing them to a character in a novel who was so busy shoveling muck in a barn that he failed to see the good things in life.

Their exposés in popular magazines such as *McClure's, Collier's,* and *Ladies' Home Journal* helped generate the grassroots support that enabled the Progressive movement to become a powerful national force. Ida Tarbell exposed tactics employed by Standard Oil to extort privileges from government, control elected officials, and crush its competitors. Lincoln Steffens examined how corrupt politicians in cities such as St. Louis and Minneapolis failed to provide citizens with decent public services. In his novel *The Jungle,* Upton Sinclair decried the exploitation of workers in a fictitious meatpacking plant.

City and State Reform

Like most American political movements, Progressivism began at the local level as early reformers attacked corrupt city governments. Progressive officials in Boston, Denver, Milwaukee, New York, Philadelphia, and San Francisco created fair methods to award government contracts, reformed hiring practices, and improved schools, transportation, sanitation, and other municipal services.

Government contracts for road construction or garbage hauling, which once went to firms that offered officials the largest bribe, were now granted through

QUICK JURGIS WE MUST RECOVER THE BODY FROM THE LARD VAT!

ALL STAR FEATURE CORP. presents IN MOTION PICTURES

— UPTON SINCLAIR'S —
WONDERFUL STORY OF THE BEEF PACKING INDUSTRY

THE JUNGLE

FEATURING

GEORGE NASH – GAIL KANE
AND THE AUTHOR
5 DARING ACTS — 210 ASTOUNDING SCENES

The Jungle, *Upton Sinclair's dramatic exposé of the meatpacking industry, was so popular it was made into a movie. His graphic descriptions of how meat was butchered and processed led to new laws to make food packaging more sanitary.*

competitive, open bidding. Instead of allowing officials to hire incompetent friends and relatives, civil service laws ensured that capable workers held government jobs. It all meant better, cleaner government for America.

One of the best-known state reformers was Robert M. "Fighting Bob" La Follette, who became governor of Wisconsin in 1900. His philosophy, known as the Wis-

consin Idea, was that government could create "a happier and better state to live in," so that "its institutions are more democratic, that the opportunities for all of its people are more equal, that social justice more nearly prevails, that human life is safer and sweeter"[4] for all citizens.

Wisconsin became a laboratory for Progressive reform by passing laws that tightened regulation of railroads and corporations, established civil service procedures, initiated the nation's first graduated income tax, and created state commissions to oversee factory safety and sanitation. Wisconsin also became the first state to establish direct primary elections, so voters could nominate candidates. In the past political parties had selected candidates for the general election, but by 1912 all but three states had direct primaries.

Also, in 1913 the Seventeenth Amendment to the Constitution was ratified, granting voters the right to elect senators instead of having state legislatures appoint them. This, too, returned power to voters.

Progressive leaders included Joseph W. Folk, elected governor after leading a fight against corruption in Missouri; New York State attorney general Charles Evans Hughes, who became governor after exposing corrupt practices of the state's powerful insurance companies; and New Jersey governor Woodrow Wilson.

After his 1910 election Wilson won approval for workers' compensation, public utility regulation, the direct primary, and other Progressive programs. Two years later this Democrat took his Progressive ideas to the national level and jousted with Theodore Roosevelt in one of history's wildest presidential campaigns.

The Election of 1912

The 1912 election featured Wilson, Republican incumbent William Howard Taft, who succeeded Roosevelt when he stepped down in 1908, and Roosevelt, whose return to politics generated the most powerful third-party drive in U.S. history. A measure of the popularity and power of the Progressive movement is that all three candidates, to varying degrees, backed its major aims and goals. Added to this already lively mix was Socialist Eugene V. Debs.

Elected vice president when President William McKinley won a second term in 1900, Roosevelt was renowned as an adventurous outdoorsman, a hero of the Spanish-American War, and a reform governor of New York. Roosevelt became president after McKinley was assassinated on September 6, 1901.

Roosevelt, the youngest of all presidents at age forty-two, became the guiding light of Progressives and was nicknamed "Trust Buster" after initiating more than forty actions to break up illegal business combinations in the railroad, oil, tobacco, beef, and sugar industries. He also intervened in a coal miners' strike in 1902 to

While governor of New Jersey, Woodrow Wilson's Progressive policies helped him win the presidential election of 1912.

help workers win a 10 percent pay hike and a nine-hour day, and strengthened the power of the Interstate Commerce Commission to regulate the railroad industry. One of the first great conservationists, while President, Roosevelt set aside more than 230 million acres of land for public ownership.

Roosevelt's vice president, Taft, a giant of a man at three hundred pounds, continued to attack trusts when elected president in 1908 and won stricter regulation of rail-

Theodore Roosevelt

Newspaper editor William Allen White once wrote, "The gift of the gods to Theodore Roosevelt was joy, joy in life. He took joy in everything he did, in hunting, campaigning, and ranching, in politics, in commanding the Rough Riders." It was his unbridled zest for life that made Roosevelt one of the most beloved presidents in history.

Born to a wealthy family in New York, "Teddy" was a sickly child who suffered from asthma. But with the same fierce determination that would help him succeed as an adult, Roosevelt lifted weights and exercised to make himself strong. He also became a voracious reader to strengthen his mind.

Roosevelt, who felt the presidency was a bully pulpit to effect change, became the first truly activist president, attacking trusts, conserving land, and trying to make the United States a world power. This whimsical poem by Rosemary and Stephen Vincent Benet quoted in *American Pageant,* shows how popular Roosevelt was with average Americans:

> T. R. is spanking a Senator, T. R. is chasing a bear,
>
> T. R. is busting an Awful Trust, And dragging it from its lair.
>
> They're calling T. R. a lot of things—The men in the private car—
>
> But the day-coach likes exciting folks, and the day-coach likes T. R.

In 1902 a new child's toy—the Teddy Bear—was named after Roosevelt. The stuffed bear got its name after Roosevelt refused to shoot and kill a trapped bear. It was an apt honor for a man who retained a youthful

Theodore Roosevelt, the "Bull Moose" party candidate for president in 1912. His features—a bushy mustache, thick glasses, and gap-toothed smile were easy targets for editorial cartoonists.

prankishness as an adult. "You must always remember," a friend, quoted in *America Enters the World,* once cautioned, "that the president is about six years old."

It was also Roosevelt who named the home the president lives in the White House; before his tenure it was called the Executive Mansion.

roads. But congressmen controlled by business interests weakened his proposal to reduce tariffs. Taft's perceived failure on tariff reduction, his ineffectiveness in other areas, and general unpopularity split the Republican Party.

When Roosevelt returned home in June 1910 after a long African safari to find the Republican Party divided and dispirited, he moved quickly to recapture the political spotlight. In a fiery speech August 31,1910, in Osawatomie, Kansas, Roosevelt introduced his New Nationalism, the successor to his original Square Deal program: "I mean not merely that I stand for fair play under the present rules of the game, but . . . for having those rules changed so as to work for a more substantial equality of opportunity and of reward for [everyone]." Roosevelt declared those changes should come "mainly through the national government."[5] He backed an eight-hour day for workers, child labor laws, and voting rights for all citizens as well as greater regulation of big business.

When Roosevelt declared in February 1912 that "my hat's in the ring! The fight is on and I'm stripped to the buff!"[6] he not only colorfully announced his candidacy but created a political metaphor still used today by candidates seeking office. Progressive Republicans rallied around their hero and in June traveled to the Republican convention in Chicago intent on nominating him. But even though Roosevelt had won more votes in primary elections, party regulars engineered a Taft nomination.

Roosevelt and other Progressives walked out in anger but returned to Chicago in August to create the National Progressive Party. They nominated Roosevelt, who contributed a colorful nickname for the new party when he bellowed to reporters, "I am as strong as a bull moose!"[7] Caricatures of a moose joined the Democratic donkey and Republican elephant as the cartoon symbol of the new party.

Wilson, who won the Democratic nomination, was more antibusiness than Roosevelt and presented a program he called the New Freedom. Demanding an end to "the curse of bigness," Wilson advocated forced limits on the size of corporations, lower tariffs, and government regulation to ensure equal economic opportunities. "If America is not to have free enterprise," Wilson said, "then she can have freedom of no sort whatever."[8]

Wilson was elected with 435 electoral votes to 88 for Roosevelt and 8 for Taft. But he was a minority president with only 41 percent of the popular vote (6.3 million) as Roosevelt (4.1 million, 27 percent) and Taft (3.5 million, 23 percent) combined to outpoll him. A political cartoon summed up the election with an equation that showed an elephant (Republicans) divided by a moose (Progressives) equaled a donkey (Democrats). Even Debs rode the swell of reformist feeling to 900,762 votes, more than double his total four years earlier.

Wilson Brings Progressive Ideas Alive

The election showed Americans were ready for real reform—and Wilson was ready to deliver. In his inaugural address he said:

Woodrow Wilson

Although Woodrow Wilson inherited the Progressive mantle from Theodore Roosevelt, the two men were as unlike as any two presidents in history.

An ascetic-looking intellectual with antique pince-nez eyeglasses perched precariously on his thin nose, Wilson's dour, aloof nature was in sharp contrast to the hearty, fun-loving Rough Rider. The son of a Presbyterian minister, Wilson was born in Virginia shortly before the Civil War and grew up in Georgia in an atmosphere of extreme piety.

After earning a Ph.D. at Johns Hopkins University, Wilson taught at several colleges including Princeton, where he became president in 1902. His reputation as a reformer helped him become New Jersey governor in 1910 and president two years later.

Frail in health for most of his life, as president, Wilson suffered from headaches and stomach problems. He was also the victim of a stroke in 1919 that incapacitated him for several months, leaving the nation without a leader.

Wilson could be harsh in dealing with people—one of his cabinet members, quoted in *America Enters the World*, characterized him as "clean, strong, high-minded and cold-blooded." He mockingly admitted to having "a vague, conjectural personality, more made up of opinions and academic prepossessions than of human traits and red corpuscles." His strong stubborn streak and sense of self-

President Woodrow Wilson at his most comfortable role—delivering a speech. He was one of the greatest orators to ever hold the nation's highest office.

righteousness made him unwilling to compromise. He once said, "I would rather fail in a cause I know some day will triumph than to win in a cause that I know some day will fail."

Like Roosevelt, Wilson believed the president should be a dynamic leader who could dictate policy to Congress. One of Wilson's greatest strengths was his ability to make dynamic, eloquent speeches, a weapon he used to win public support in his attempts to make Congress bend to his will.

We have been proud of our industrial achievements but we have not hitherto stopped thoughtfully enough to count the human cost, the cost of lives snuffed out, of energies overtaxed and broken, the fearful physical and spiritual cost to the men and women and children on whom the dead weight and burden of it all has fallen pitilessly the years through.[9]

Wilson then began his assault on what he called the "triple wall of privilege"[10]—the tariff, the U.S. banking and currency system, and trusts. His first act was to call

Congress into special session on tariffs, and he got quick results. In October 1913 Congress passed the Underwood Tariff Act, the first downward revision of tariffs in almost two decades and the largest since before the Civil War. Products such as food, wool, iron, and steel were placed on the free list (they were produced more cheaply in America anyway) while rates on many other items were substantially reduced. U.S. firms would now have to compete with foreign countries.

Lower federal revenue from reduced tariffs forced Congress to enact the nation's first personal income tax, which had become legal in February 1913 with ratifica-

tion of the Sixteenth Amendment to the Constitution. The graduated tax varied from 1 percent to 6 percent but applied only to corporations and a small proportion of Americans who earned more than $4,000 annually. Although the tax had minimal impact—a married worker making $5,000 a year paid $10—it was historic because it marked a major shift in the source of federal revenue. The U.S. government traditionally had been funded through tariffs, fees for use of public lands, and taxes on alcohol.

Two months later Congress passed the Federal Reserve Bank Act, creating a central federal bank and twelve regional banks

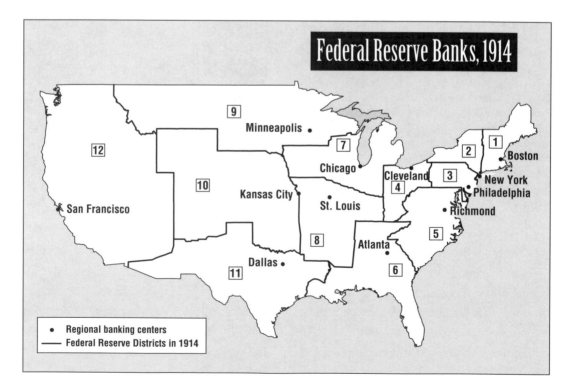

Federal Reserve Banks, 1914

- Regional banking centers
— Federal Reserve Districts in 1914

that were controlled by the Federal Reserve Board. The board regulated credit and the nation's money supply by setting the interest rate it charged member banks, by buying and selling government bonds, and by issuing paper currency. Wilson said the new system would free banking from control of what was called the Money Trust "so that the banks may be the instruments, not the masters of business and of individual enterprise and initiative."[11]

A financial panic in 1907 had proven the need for a central bank to control the money supply and to take away control from financiers such as Morgan. The bill authorized the Federal Reserve Bank to issue Federal Reserve notes, backed by gold reserves, which allowed it to expand or contract the supply of currency as necessary.

And Wilson did not forget about trusts. In 1914 he created the Federal Trade Commission to oversee business activity. The commission had the authority to review proposed business mergers and other transactions and rule on whether they violated rules against formation of unfair business combinations. The FTC could also investigate established companies for violations of such rules.

That same year Wilson helped win passage of the Clayton Antitrust Act, which strengthened the little-used Sherman Antitrust Act, which for several decades had been ineffective in dealing with big business. It outlawed key corporate practices that gave businesses unfair economic advantages, including price discrimination, which allowed firms to give selected customers unfair price breaks, and formation of holding companies and interlocking directorates, which enabled companies to operate like trusts.

The Clayton Antitrust Act was important for unions because it legalized strikes, picketing, and boycotts, their main weapons. It also exempted unions from antitrust laws, which businesses had used to prosecute striking workers. Samuel Gompers, founder of the American Federation of Labor, the nation's largest union, hailed the provision as an important new freedom for American workers.

In 1916 Wilson tackled a new series of Progressive measures. In January he nominated liberal reformer Louis Brandeis to the Supreme Court, the first Jew to serve on the high court; signed the Farm Loan Act to create federal land banks to ease rural credit; approved the Federal Child Labor Law; and won congressional approval of the Adamson Act, which mandated eight-hour days for railroad workers. He also supported a bill to protect the rights and working conditions of merchant seamen and helped pass measures to ensure farmers cheap, long-term credit and to provide more federal aid to schools and for highway construction.

Those efforts helped Wilson win reelection in 1916 over Republican Charles

Evans Hughes, although the contest was decided as much on U.S. involvement in World War I as on Progressive issues. Although the United States did not enter the conflict until 1917, three years after it began, the war had increasingly become the number one issue facing the United States.

The End of the Progressive Era

By the end of his first term Wilson's proud boast was that he had made good on virtually all the major goals of both the Progressive and Democratic Parties. The problems facing the nation at the turn of the century, however, were not gone; rather, they had only been alleviated by the actions taken by Roosevelt, Wilson, and elected officials on the state and local level.

The Progressive movement, however, began to fade after 1916, eclipsed by World War I as the focus of Americans' attention. For the first time in the nation's history, Americans became more concerned with events in Europe than in their own country. Increasingly, they feared what the war would mean for America.

Chapter Two

Immigrant workers from the Erie City Iron Works assemble for an Americanization class after finishing their work day, circa 1910. These new Americans and others, many unable to speak English and unfamiliar with the nation's democratic traditions, had to fight their own battle to win on-the-job rights.

The Fight for Rights

On March 25, 1911, the five hundred employees of the Triangle Shirtwaist Company had been working since dawn making shirtwaists, the tailored blouses worn by fashionable women. They were among thirty thousand New York garment workers who hand-sewed clothing in more than six hundred crowded, dingy "sweatshops." The average pay for a fifty-six-hour week was $6.

When a fire broke out on the eighth floor of the ten-floor Asch Building, it became a death trap. Many fire escapes were broken, the elevators stopped running, and doors were kept locked so workers could not leave before their shift was over. Scores of workers, some with their hair and clothes on fire, others maddened by fear as the fire spread, jumped out of windows as high as the tenth floor. "Spectators," said one newspaper account, "saw again and again pitiable companionships formed in the instant of death—girls who placed their arms around each other as they leaped." [12]

Bodies line the sidewalk in front of the Asch building in New York City. The fire in the building claimed the lives of 146 Triangle Shirtwaist Company workers and sparked the development of reforms in worker safety regulations.

One hundred and forty-six workers died of burns or smoke inhalation. A few days later a quarter of a million people watched eighty thousand protesters march in silent tribute to the dead workers, victims of an unsafe workplace. The owners of the firm were acquitted of charges of manslaughter but the blaze forced New York State officials to investigate working conditions in the garment industry. The four-year-long probe led to the most far-reaching labor code of its time, including state laws that created fire safety regulations, limited work-ing hours, and prohibited children under fourteen from working.

Progressives Ignore Some Problems

In 1910 millions of unskilled workers like those at the Triangle Shirtwaist Company labored ten to twelve hours a day, six or seven days a week for less than $10, barely enough to feed their families even though bread was 6 cents a loaf and milk 18 cents a gallon. Millions of immigrants lived in poverty and were increasingly rejected by their fellow Americans. More than 90 percent of the nation's 9 million blacks lived in the South, where they were denied their civil rights. Women could not vote and were not equal to men under the nation's laws.

The Progressive movement did much to improve the lives of many embattled Americans. But many Progressives ignored racial injustice, anti-Semitism, and persecution of immigrants, and only halfheartedly supported women's rights. And although Progressives helped workers in many ways, their support of the struggling labor unions was lukewarm. Thus in the early twentieth century many groups had to wage individual fights for rights and justice.

The Labor Movement

Labor unions emerged after the Civil War in direct response to the machines and factories of the Industrial Revolution, which had replaced glassblowers, gunsmiths, shoemakers, and weavers. Unskilled workers performing simple tasks could now mass-produce products that artisans and skilled workers had once made by hand. Now workers could be hired for minimal wages, were easily replaced, and had little leverage in dealing with their employers. The founders of the American Federation of Labor (AFL), the first successful national union, explained this historic shift in the role and status of American workers:

The various trades have been affected by the introduction of machinery, the subdivision of labor, the use of women's and children's labor and the lack of an apprentice system, so that the skilled trades were rapidly sinking to the level of pauper labor.[13]

The AFL continues today in the form of the AFL-CIO (American Federation of Labor–Congress of Industrial Organizations). The AFL was created in 1886 as a loose confederation of local unions representing about 140,000 skilled workers in trades such as carpentry, masonry, and cigar making. It was the successor to the failed Noble Order of the Knights of Labor, which began in 1869 but failed to become a powerful national union. Samuel L. Gompers, a cigar maker from New York, headed the AFL for all but one year from 1886 to his death in 1924.

The growth of the AFL and other unions was slow; by 1916 the AFL had only 2 million members and only 10 percent of American workers were represented by unions. Management, usually with the backing of the courts and local officials, was largely successful in fighting union organization.

A rival to the AFL was the radical Industrial Workers of the World (IWW), whose members were nicknamed Wobblies. The IWW was founded in 1905 by Socialists and other political radicals including William "Big Bill" Haywood, a western miner who headed the new union. Haywood stated IWW's goal was to "con-

Mother Jones and the Labor Movement

Dressed like a society matron with the white hair, wire-rim glasses, and plump face of a grandmother, Mary Harris Jones looked like anything but what she was—a volatile, radical supporter of the labor movement.

Nicknamed "Mother Jones," she became a legend in the labor movement when she began fighting for acceptance of unions such as the United Mine Workers. She also helped found the radical Industrial Workers of the World.

Born in Ireland in 1830, she immigrated to America and taught school in Michigan and Memphis, Tennessee, before marrying an ironworker in 1861. Six years later, after her husband and their four children died of yellow fever during an epidemic in Memphis, she moved to Chicago and opened a dressmaking shop.

Mary Harris "Mother" Jones chats amiably with President Calvin Coolidge. An immigrant from Ireland, Jones was a fiery and legendary figure in the fight to establish the rights of labor in her adopted homeland.

When the Chicago fire of 1871 destroyed her business, she turned to the Knights of Labor for help. Impressed by what the Knights had done for her, she became a union organizer. Her slogan was "Join the union, boys," but Mother Jones also liked to advise people to "pray for the dead and fight like hell for the living."

Once in West Virginia she walked up to a gunman hired by a coal company to oppose striking mineworkers. When he pointed his rifle at her, Mother Jones put her hand on the muzzle and said, "Shoot an old woman if you dare!" He did not dare but authorities in West Virginia threw her in jail in 1902 and again in 1913, when she was eighty-three. She was also jailed in Colorado in 1913 and 1914 for leading miners' strikes.

Jones, who lived until 1930, was still going strong during the strikes by steelworkers after World War I in 1919 when she appeared in Gary, Indiana, to encourage workers. "We're going to take over the steel mills and run them for Uncle Sam," she said to their cheers.

federate the workers of this country into a working-class movement that shall have for its purpose the emancipation of the working class from the slave bondage of capitalism."[14] The AFL, by contrast, was not opposed to capitalism—it only wanted workers to receive more of its financial rewards.

IWW membership peaked at about fifty thousand members, mostly migrant workers in wheat fields, lumberjacks, and metal miners in western states. The union failed to gain widespread acceptance because of its radical philosophy and use of violence, including the murder of opponents. The IWW was effectively destroyed during World War I because the federal government prosecuted so many of its leaders for opposing the war and because so many Americans turned against it for the same reason.

Socialists and Other Radicals

Many more radical labor advocates turned to socialism after the depression of 1893, which left thousands of working poor jobless, homeless, and desperate. Angered that

Workers in 1914 gather for a protest organized by the Industrial Workers of the World. A partially obscured sign in the background that reads "HUNGER" explains the goal of this radical labor group—to improve economic conditions for workers.

government officials had done nothing to ease their plight, some Americans turned to Marxist socialism, a political theory formulated in Europe in the mid–nineteenth century by Karl Marx and Friedrich Engels. Marx's ideas also became the basis of communism; socialism in America, however, was advanced as a democratic and not totalitarian form of government.

Socialism was opposed to capitalism, the American economic system in which the means of production and distribution are privately owned. Socialists claimed capitalism was the cause of modern problems for workers because it pitted them and owners in an economic struggle. Socialism instead advocated government ownership and control of the economy so all citizens could share the financial rewards.

This was a stark departure from the thinking of even the most liberal Progressives, who never challenged the fundamental principles of capitalism. Socialism won many converts, especially in the labor movement, who believed America's economic and political system had failed them.

By 1912 the Socialist Party claimed more than a hundred thousand members, more than a thousand local elected officials were Socialist Party members, including fifty-six mayors, and one Socialist had been elected to Congress. Socialist mayors

Ford Hikes Pay

On January 14, 1914, automaker Henry Ford did something the *New York Sun* said was "unheard of in the history of business"—he voluntarily raised the pay of his employees. In fact, Ford sent wages skyrocketing to the unheard-of sum of $5 a day!

Unlike other big businessmen of his time, Ford decided to share the profits he was making with his thirteen thousand workers. The average wage for skilled workers at the time was $2 a day, but the new $5 minimum covered even unskilled workers and the workday at the Ford plant in Detroit was only eight hours. The day after his announcement twelve thousand people applied for jobs.

Historian Mark Sullivan writes in volume 4 of *Our Times* that Ford introduced a "revolution in economic thought and practice." Ford had decided to treat his workers "not according to the Adam Smith concepts, as ones to be hired at the lowest wages they can be persuaded to accept, not as ones to leave with the employer the largest possible share of the fruits of industry, but as ones to be paid high wages in order that they might become maximum consumers of the goods Ford and others had to sell."

It was a revolutionary idea and few other business executives were willing to treat their workers as royally as Ford. This left Ford's lucky employees with some of the highest-paying, best jobs in America. A poem in the *Detroit Free Press*, quoted in *Our Times*, volume 4, summed up the reaction of Ford workers:

Of all glad words,
That now are roared,
The gladdest are these:
He works for Ford.

adopted civil service and other Progressive reforms, fought government corruption, and worked hard to improve services to all citizens.

Communists and anarchists, whose beliefs were even more radical than socialism, remained a political fringe in the decade.

Immigrants

These new more radical political theories, as well as the basic ideas underlying the labor movement, were brought to the United States by the millions of immigrants who flooded the nation in the late nineteenth century and early twentieth century. Gompers, for example, was a native of England and a member of a craft trade before he immigrated.

Arriving at the rate of nearly a million a year from 1900 to 1914, almost all of the new immigrants moved to big cities in search of work. But they had another battle to fight besides finding a job—prejudice.

Until 1880 three-fourths of the immigrants, sometimes called the "first wave," were from the British Isles, Germany, and Scandinavia, with the largest contingents coming from Ireland and Germany. "Second wave" immigrants were mostly from Italy, Poland, Russia, Austria-Hungary, and other southern and eastern European countries.

Members of this family from Hungary are among the nearly 14 million immigrants who flooded into America between 1900 and 1914. This "second wave" of immigrants, mainly from eastern Europe, were often seen as inferior because they had different languages, religions, and customs than previous immigrants.

The newer immigrants were rejected because they brought with them languages, customs, and religions that seemed strange to many Americans. Many of the new arrivals to predominantly Protestant America were Jewish and Catholic.

Because almost all immigrants moved to big cities, their great numbers began to dramatically change the ethnic makeup of those cities and many people began to fear they would change the quality of American life. Among them was President Woodrow Wilson.

"Through the century men of the sturdy stocks of the North of Europe had made up the mainstream of foreign blood which was every year added to the vital force of the country," Wilson wrote in his 1902 book *A History of the American People*:

> Now there came multitudes of men of the lowest class from the South of Italy and men of the meaner sort out of Hungary and Poland, men out of the ranks where there was neither skill nor energy nor any initiative of quick intelligence. [It was as if] the countries of the south of Europe were disburdening themselves of the more sordid and hapless elements of their populations. Even the Chinese were more to be desired . . . than most of the coarse crew that came forward every year at the eastern ports.[15]

Although most Americans at the turn of the century were only just beginning to feel antagonism toward immigrants, the nation had already shut its doors to Asians. The Chinese Exclusion Act of 1882, which was made permanent in 1902, barred immigration from China and in 1906 Japan and the United States had agreed to prohibit immigration by unskilled laborers. These restrictions were forced by the "yellow peril" racial fears that white Americans harbored about the large number of Asians coming to the West Coast.

Americans now similarly began to fear and reject newer immigrants, making it harder for them to find jobs and gain acceptance. The result was that they banded together in urban enclaves where others from their former homelands lived. They felt safe in such neighborhoods, often called "Chinatown" or "Little Italy" depending on their ethnic makeup, because residents all shared a common language, religion, and customs, and the security of familiar routines and goods.

Because so many immigrants were poor, the areas where they lived became the first urban slums; millions lived in tenements, large buildings in which an entire family might live in one small room. The tenements were poorly constructed, foul smelling because of lack of ventilation and adequate sanitary facilities, and usually in need of repair.

With no political power, wealth, or education to fight back, immigrants banded together in various ethnic social clubs or societies. These organizations helped immigrants secure proper medical treatment and aided them in many other ways.

Immigrants were also aided by the settlement house movement that emerged at the end of the nineteenth century. Hull House in Chicago, opened in 1889 by Jane Addams, was one of the first to feed and clothe newcomers while teaching them English and helping them become accustomed to American ways. By 1900 there were more than one hundred settlement houses in big cities. They were vitally needed because government did little to help the poor and needy.

Labor Strife

The massive influx of immigrants and rural Americans into big cities created a surplus of labor that gave workers even less bargaining power. Workers tried to organize unions to gain leverage in negotiating with management but owners used their wealth and political influence to fight unionization. Management claimed unions were illegal because they violated antitrust laws and hired thugs to beat up workers who

Jane Addams and Hull House

Jane Addams grew up in middle-class comfort, the daughter of a banker in Cedarville, Illinois. But she devoted her life to helping poor immigrants by founding Hull House in Chicago, one of the first settlement houses in the nation.

The settlement house movement helped people by teaching them to read and write and offering them food, medical care, and other social services. They filled a gap because governments did very little in this era to help the poor. By 1900 there were one hundred settlement houses and by 1910 more than four hundred; Hull House was the most famous, gaining a worldwide reputation.

Addams learned about settlement houses in London in the late 1880s when she toured Europe after graduating from the Rockford Female Seminary. With a friend, Ellen Gates Starr, Addams bought the decaying Hull Mansion on Chicago's west side in 1889 and turned it into a center to help immigrants.

At Hull House, Germans, Italians, Russians, and people from other countries learned to speak English, to read and write, and to understand the customs and laws of their new country.

Although revered for her work with the poor, Addams, a confirmed pacifist who was the first international president of the Women's International League for Peace and Freedom, was harshly criticized for opposing U.S.

Jane Addams, founder of Hull House in Chicago, was a leader of the settlement house movement and devoted her life to helping immigrants adapt to life in America.

participation in World War I. In 1931 she became the first American woman to win the Nobel Peace Prize.

joined unions or went on strike. Railroad magnate Jay Gould once said, "I can hire one-half of the working class to kill the other half."[16]

The battle between management and unions became so bitter that in 1912 President William Taft created the Commission on Industrial Relations. The nine members of the commission (three each representing the public, employees, and employers) issued a report (which did little but highlight the problem) after holding hearings for 154 days. Commission chairman Frank Walsh, a Kansas City lawyer and reformer, asked a key question in the report: "Have the workers received a fair share of the enormous increase in wealth which has taken place in this country as a result largely of their labors? The answer is emphatically No!" Walsh said most workers lived in marginal conditions and "about one-third were living in a state which can only be described as abject poverty." The report concluded that labor-management relations were such a severe problem that "since the year 1877 it has frequently resulted practically in civil war."[17]

The major confrontations between labor and management came during strikes, when workers quit working to demand higher pay, better working conditions, or the right to be represented by a union. One of the most important was in 1912 in the textile mills of Lawrence, Massachusetts, which employed twenty-five thousand of the city's eighty-five thousand residents. After the state passed a law in January reducing the workweek from fifty-six to fifty-four hours, owners cut wages $3\frac{1}{2}$ percent. For the lowest-paid workers, who averaged only $6 a week, the reduction meant starvation.

Although the AFL and IWW represented only a few thousand workers, all the workers in the mills struck and the walkout spread to more than 250,000 workers in Massachusetts and neighboring states. During the bitter six-week dispute, some strikers were shot to death and others were beaten. Rising public outcry forced owners to negotiate with the strikers, who eventually won higher pay and shorter hours.

Conditions for workers slowly improved in the first half of the second decade. Progressive legislation on the state and federal level limited hours, improved safety conditions, provided for the welfare of injured and older workers, and eased some restrictions on unions that helped them organize workers.

For workers in unions the average industrial wage rose from $17.57 a week in 1890 to $23.98 in 1915 and their average workweek fell from 54.4 hours to 48.9. Nonunion workers saw their average wages increase during the same period from $8.82 to $11.52 while their workweek declined from 62.2 hours to 55.6.

Blacks

The plight of black workers was even worse. Blacks did not get much support from Progressives or Wilson, who blacks helped elect in 1912 after he promised to help them. Instead, Wilson betrayed them as president.

The Virginia-born Wilson appointed many southerners to his staff, including Postmaster General Albert S. Burleson. At a cabinet meeting on April 11, 1913, Burleson recommended segregating black federal workers. Wilson did not object and soon after that black and white federal workers were ordered to use separate lunchrooms and restrooms. When the National Association for the Advancement of Colored People (NAACP), criticized the segregation, Wilson said: "I honestly believe segregation to be in the interest of the colored people as exempting them from friction and criticism."[18]

Wilson also appointed whites to diplomatic positions in Haiti and the Dominican Republic that had traditionally been reserved for blacks. Black activist Booker T. Washington said he had never seen his people so "discouraged and embittered."[19]

Blacks were treated worse than any other group in America. The 8 million blacks who resided in southern states lived under Jim Crow laws that kept them segregated and took away other civil rights. Blacks also lived in fear of racist violence; in the first fifteen years of the twentieth century more than a thousand blacks were lynched, burned, or shot to death.

Born a slave in 1856 on a farm in Vir-

Booker T. Washington was born a slave in 1856 in Virginia but went on to found the Tuskegee Institute, one of the first schools dedicated to teaching black students. At the turn of the century Washington was the most influential black leader in America as well as the first to visit the White House and meet with President Theodore Roosevelt.

ginia, Booker T. Washington founded the Tuskegee Institute, a school in Alabama that taught black students industrial arts. Washington backed a policy of "accommodation" in which blacks accepted segregation while working hard to gain future acceptance by whites.

Washington believed if blacks could learn trades and make money, their economic power would help them to achieve equality with whites. But he has been criticized for his willingness to accept segregation and not demand the right to vote and other civil rights for blacks. "It is at the bottom of life we must start, not at the top," Washington said. "In all things that are purely social we can be as separate as the fingers, yet one as the hand in all things essential to mutual progress."[20] When he would say this, Washington would hold up his hand, fingers spread apart, and then close his hand into a fist.

In the twentieth century Washington's tactics were challenged by the NAACP. Its leader, W. E. B. (William Edward Burghardt) Du Bois, a fiery orator and eloquent writer, helped found the landmark civil rights organization in 1909. Du Bois was editor of the *Crisis*, the group's monthly journal, and in 1910 became the NAACP's director. The first black to earn a master's from Harvard, he refused to accept the status quo and urged blacks to demand their rights immediately: "The way for a people to gain their reasonable rights is not by voluntarily throwing them away." In *The Souls of Black Folk*, Du Bois said blacks must realize that "voting is necessary to modern manhood, that discrimination is

barbarism, and that black boys need education as well as white boys."[21] Du Bois believed higher education would help blacks in their fight for equality.

Du Bois brought a new force to the fight for civil rights, but it would be many decades before blacks would achieve equal treatment in America.

Women's Suffrage

Nineteenth-century perceptions of the role of women still dominated the second decade of the new century. Women, that is, should be content to be wives and mothers and subservient to men; they had no need for higher education or the right to vote. This attitude, held by most women at the time as well as by men, resulted in unfair treatment in many ways. In most states women were unable to own property or make legal decisions and were restricted in the jobs they could hold. The few women who went to college usually wound up working as teachers or secretaries because they were not welcome in most professions.

Women who chafed under these conditions decided that the best way to fight for more equal treatment was to win the right to vote. Although by 1910 the suffrage movement was more than a half-century old, women could still vote in only four states—Colorado, Idaho, Utah, and Wyoming.

Led by the National American Woman Suffrage Association (NAWSA), women in

W. E. B. Du Bois

William Edward Burghardt (W. E. B.) Du Bois was the early twentieth century's most important civil rights leader. An eloquent speaker and writer, his words, quoted in *America Enters the World,* even today carry the ring of prophecy and strength of purpose that were among his greatest gifts.

"The problem of the 20th Century," Du Bois said in 1900, "is the problem of the color line; the question as to how far differences of race . . . will hereafter be made the basis of denying to over half the world the right of sharing to their utmost ability the opportunities and privileges of modern civilization." His statement came at a time when blacks in America were lynched and beaten, denied the right to vote, and segregated by law.

Du Bois, who in 1909 helped found the National Association for the Advancement of Colored People (NAACP), grew up in Great Barrington, Massachusetts, of mixed African and European ancestry. He attended Fisk University in Nashville, Tennessee, for several years and in 1890 was admitted to Harvard, where he became the first black to earn a doctorate.

It was in Tennessee where Du Bois first encountered racism. "I saw the race hatred of the whites as I had never dreamed of it before—naked and unashamed. The faint discrimination of my hopes and desires paled into nothing before this great, red monster of cruel oppression," he wrote in *The Souls of Black Folk.*

His experience forged a resolve to fight for equality for blacks, but Du Bois did not preach hatred of whites. In a quote from *America Enters the World*, in 1904 he wrote:

Originator of the phrase "black is beautiful," W. E. B. Du Bois was a fiery advocate for civil rights.

"I believe in God who made of one blood all races that dwell on earth. I believe that all men, black and brown, and white, are brothers, varying, through Time and Opportunity, in form and gift and feature, but differing in no essential particular, and alike in soul and in the possibility of infinite development."

Credited as the originator of the phrase "black is beautiful," Du Bois also believed blacks should take pride in themselves. "Especially," he wrote, "do I believe in the Negro race: in the beauty of its genius, the sweetness of its soul."

the second decade stepped up their campaign, holding rallies, giving speeches, lobbying Congress, and parading in great numbers. In 1912 some fifteen thousand women marched down Fifth Avenue in New York and three years later in the same city forty thousand protested their inability to vote.

Progressives did not always support the women's movement. In 1908 President

Theodore Roosevelt said he was not an "enthusiastic advocate" because "I do not think giving the women suffrage will produce any marked improvement in the condition for women."[22] Wilson did not back women's suffrage until 1918.

NAWSA's philosophy of trying to win the right to vote on a state-by-state basis began to show results as more and more states granted women the vote, including California in 1911 and Illinois in 1913. Women finally won the right to vote nationally in 1920.

World War I Changes Everything

The conditions under which all these groups lived, however, would soon undergo a dramatic change. Although the United States did not enter World War I

Women from around the nation travel to Washington, D.C., in February 1913, to march for the right to vote. Suffragettes battled for more than a half century before passage of the Nineteenth Amendment to the Constitution in 1920 finally granted them that basic right.

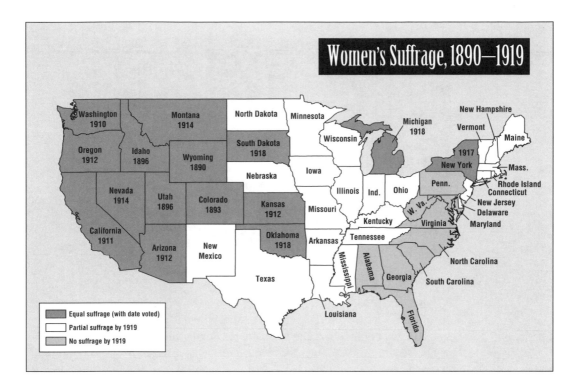

Women's Suffrage, 1890–1919

Equal suffrage (with date voted)
Partial suffrage by 1919
No suffrage by 1919

until 1917, the 1914 outbreak of war immediately began to create massive changes in American life.

The booming war economy created thousands of good, new jobs for workers, including opportunities for women and blacks in professions previously closed to them. The war led to a dramatic shift in population as blacks migrated by the hundreds of thousands to northern cities. Immigrants whose homelands fought against the United States were discriminated against and distrusted and there was a general increase in anti-immigrant sentiment. Socialists and other radicals, who generally opposed the war, were suspected of being traitors and many were jailed.

The war meant that life would never be the same again for any of these groups.

Chapter Three

In 1910, movies were becoming one of the most popular forms of amusement in America. By the end of the decade silent movies would surpass vaudeville as the most popular mass entertainment in the nation.

Popular Culture: Silent Films, Vaudeville, and the Model T

The first flickering images that crawled across makeshift screens in the second decade of the twentieth century marked the beginning of one of the world's most powerful mediums of mass communication—the motion picture.

During the 1910s silent movies grew

from a curiosity to one of America's most popular types of entertainment. More importantly, they became the nation's first mass medium as people in New York or Los Angeles, Miami or Milwaukee, Detroit or Denver could laugh together over the antics of comedian Charlie Chaplin or swoon over the beauty of Mary Pickford.

Because radio and television had not yet been invented, there was no simultaneous dissemination of information and entertainment to the entire nation. People got the news from local newspapers, sometimes days after an important event had occurred. Popular songs made their way slowly across the country through performances by touring entertainers in vaudeville and by the sale of sheet music.

Movies were important as the first cultural phenomenon all Americans could experience at the same time and in the same way. But motion pictures were just one way that modern technology was beginning to change American culture. The automobile was replacing the horse as a means of transportation; people could now talk coast-to-coast by telephone; and the airplane was soaring beyond novelty status.

The Birth of Motion Pictures

In 1891 Thomas Alva Edison, the inventor of the lightbulb, perfected the technology of moving pictures, and between 1891 and 1895 his company produced a number of very short films of a minute or less. Their content was common scenes such as a train rushing by or waves crashing on a beach; the very first film was of a man sneezing! Although their interest is hard to comprehend today, at the time they were such a novelty that people eagerly paid to see them.

At first films had to be viewed individually on another of Edison's inventions, the kinetoscope, a machine with a light source and a peephole through which people watched the moving pictures. In the late 1890s improved technology enabled films to be projected on a screen, and the entertainment became even more popular. By 1905 people were watching movies in nickelodeons, the first movie theaters; their name came from the nickel price of admission.

The first movie theaters were known as nickelodeons because the price of admission was a nickel. Nickelodeons in the century's early years, like the Waco Theatre shown here in this 1908 photograph, began in vacant storefront businesses that were converted to show this new form of entertainment.

Nickelodeons were usually vacant storefronts or large rented rooms that seated several hundred people. This is how the *New York Herald* newspaper described them in 1908:

> In almost every case a long, narrow room formerly used for legitimate business purposes has been made over into what is popularly known as a "nickelodeon." At the rear a stage is raised. Across it is swung a white curtain. Before the curtain is placed a piano, which does service for an orchestra. Packed into the room as closely as they can be placed are chairs for the spectators, who number from one to four hundred.[23]

The debut in 1903 of *The Great Train Robbery,* the first movie to tell a story, changed films forever. Film companies began producing comedies, dramas, adventure stories, and cowboy movies that by 1910 were luring 26 million people each week to some 10,000 nickelodeons. To help tell the story, dialogue and captions were printed on the screen. Musicians in the theater, from a piano player to a full orchestra, might accompany the action. By 1916, 25 million people a day were going to the movies and people now watched in actual movie theaters, which began appearing in 1912.

The first films were short one- or two-reel productions that lasted only a few minutes, but moviemakers gradually turned to longer, more ambitious works. The most famous feature film of the silent era was director D. W. Griffith's *Birth of A Nation* (1915), an epic about the Civil War and its aftermath in the South.

The film is considered revolutionary for Griffith's pioneering technical innovation such as the flashback, the close-up, and the fadeout. Modern-day critics have condemned the film for its racist content; based on a novel by Thomas Dixon called *The Clansman*, it portrayed members of the vigilante Ku Klux Klan as heroes while depicting blacks in a demeaning way. Hugely successful when released, the movie made more than $10 million by the end of the decade. It was also the first shown in the White House.

Hollywood and Stars

The earliest movies were made in New York City, but in 1909 film companies began moving to California to take advantage of its pleasant climate and stunning scenery. Studios sprouted up in a quiet country town near Los Angeles whose name would become synonymous with the glamour of movies—Hollywood.

Studios at first did not credit actors, but when IMP Studio began putting their names on the screen in 1910, fans began to idolize their favorites. Tom Mix, a Rough Rider in the Spanish-American War, and William S. Hart were the first cowboy stars, while Charlie Chaplin and Roscoe "Fatty" Arbuckle delighted audiences in

Mary Pickford, one of the first great movie stars, was affectionately called "Little Mary" by her millions of fans. Her popularity helped her earn $1 million a year by the end of the century's second decade.

comic roles. Douglas Fairbanks starred in swashbuckling adventure films and Mary Pickford was "Little Mary," the romantic heroine a nation fell in love with. The beautiful Clara Bow was the "It Girl," and Theda Bara became "the Vamp," the sexy bad girl men could not resist.

Actors' salaries, only about $5 a day when they were anonymous, began to skyrocket as fans clamored to see stars they liked. By 1916 Pickford and Chaplin each earned $10,000 a week; by the end of the decade $1 million a year. In 1916 *Picture*

Play, a fan magazine, criticized the salary explosion as

> without a doubt the greatest drain on the producers' bank accounts. This can be readily realized when one brings to mind the single man who draws a salary that is nearly seven times that of the president of the United States—Charlie Chaplin. Mr. Chaplin costs the Mutual company $520,000 a year.[24]

Vaudeville

Vaudeville, however, remained America's most popular form of mass entertainment until the 1930s, when movies surpassed it in the hearts of Americans. Fred Allen, a comedian who later starred on radio, wrote that

> vaudeville was the popular entertainment of the masses. Nomadic tribes of nondescript players roamed the land. The vaudeville actor was part gypsy and part suitcase. With his brash manner, flashy clothes, cape and cane . . . the vaudevillian brought happiness and excitement to the communities he visited.[25]

Derived from the French word *vaudevire*, meaning a popular satirical song, vaudeville shows were live revues combining everything from comedians, singers, jugglers, escape artists, acrobats, and jugglers to dancing elephants. Admission prices ranged from a nickel to a dollar, depending on the status of the performers. People knew that the show would have comedians, singers, and dancers but they might also see legendary escape artist Harry Houdini struggle free from chains and handcuffs or watch an animal act like Swayne's Cats and Rats, which featured rats mounted on cats who raced against each other.

The Little Tramp

Charlie Chaplin did not become a movie star until he became the Little Tramp.

The silent screen era's biggest star was born in London to a poor family of vaudeville performers. In 1913 he was touring the United States with a comic singing group when director Mack Sennett signed him to make films for Keystone productions.

Chaplin began as a bit player in 1914's *Making a Living* and in one year made thirty-five two-reel films. But it was not until the next year in *Kid Auto Races in Venice* that he created the Little Tramp, the character that made him world famous.

The Little Tramp was a woeful little figure wearing baggy pants, a coat that was too small, a derby hat that kept falling off, and a silly little mustache that barely covered the front of his upper lip. He also had the most famous walk in movie history, a curious waddling motion in which he rocked back and forth from one foot to the other and appeared to be constantly in danger of falling over. Chaplin achieved the effect by wearing a pair of oversize boots on the wrong feet. The character's only touch of grace was a cane, which he deftly twirled and used in self-defense against his adversaries, who were always several times his size.

Moviegoers fell in love with this simple, gentle soul because he represented the common man. They identified with his heartaches

Charlie Chaplin, shown with costar Edna Purviance in this scene from the silent movie Work, *created the character of the lovable Little Tramp.*

and pulled for him to survive the comedic challenges he faced. Chaplin made them laugh with clever slapstick comedy and amazing facial expressions.

Chaplin in real life became a king. In his first four years in the movies his salary went from $150 a week to $10,000 and in 1918 he signed a contract for $1 million a year, later cofounding United Artists studio. "I could never have found such success in England," Chaplin was quoted as saying years later in *Remembering Charlie* by Jerry Epstein. "This is truly the land of opportunity."

George M. Cohan, an entertainer and songwriter who became an important director of Broadway musicals, performed in vaudeville as did most of the famous singers and actors of the era. Many popular songs were first introduced in vaudeville.

Comedy stars like Ed Wynn, Eddie Cantor, Will Rogers, Fanny Brice, and the Four Marx Brothers (Chico, Harpo, Groucho, and Zeppo, who replaced a fifth brother, Gummo) kept the nation laughing. The humor was simple and silly, like this typical exchange between two of the Marx Brothers (in the movies they made in later years Harpo, a master of pantomime, never spoke):

Groucho: What is the shape of the world?

Harpo: I don't know.

Groucho: Well, what shape are my cufflinks?

Harpo: Square.

Groucho: Not my weekday cufflinks, the ones I wear on Sundays.

Harpo: Oh, round.

Groucho: All right, what is the shape of the world?

Harpo: Square on weekdays, round on Sundays.[26]

Also popular were black entertainers such as Bill "Bojangles" Robinson, the greatest tap dancer of his time, and singer Ethel Waters. White singers and dancers also performed in blackface, a southern minstrel show tradition in which whites mimicked blacks.

The last hurrah for vaudeville came in the late forties and early fifties when vaudeville greats such as Milton Berle, George Burns and Gracie Allen, Ed Wynn, and Jimmy Durante came back to become some of the first stars of television.

New Types of Music

In the twentieth century Americans were able to enjoy music in a new way by listening to records on Victrolas, phonographs cranked by hand. Popular songs in the 1910s included "Melancholy Baby," "By the Sea (By the Beautiful Sea)," and "Sweetheart of Sigma Chi." The war years created hit tunes like "How You Gonna Keep 'Em down on the Farm (After They've Seen Paree?)" and Hawaiian hits like "On the Beach at Waikiki" and "Song of the Islands."

But the most important music of the new century reflected the emergence of distinctly American forms of music like ragtime, jazz, and the blues, with roots in black spirituals and gospel music. Ragtime tunes became popular in the 1890s while the blues and jazz emerged in the twentieth century's second decade. The two most famous ragtime tunes are Scott Joplin's "Maple Leaf Rag" in 1899 and Irving Berlin's "Alexander's Ragtime Band" in 1911.

W. C. Handy is credited in 1912 with writing the first blues tune, the "St. Louis Blues." "I saw lightning strike," Handy wrote of the first time he played the song. "The dancers seemed electrified. Something within them came suddenly to life. An instinct that wanted so much to live, to fling its arms and to spread joy, took them by the heels." Handy said in the blues he tried to combine "ragtime syncopation with a real melody in the spiritual tradition" and to use "all that is characteristic of the Negro from Africa to Alabama."[27] The blues grew out of "field hollers," rhythmic songs black plantation workers sang as they worked. The blues are filled with the discouragement, disappointment, and bitterness of life so many blacks experienced.

Composer W. C. Handy makes notations on sheet music for "St. Louis Blues," his most famous song. Written in 1912, it is credited with being the first blues tune ever written.

It is believed the word jazz was used for the first time in 1917 to refer to a fast-paced Dixieland style that included a mix of slow blues and traditional black funeral music. Except for folk songs and black spirituals, Americans had always looked to Europe for their musical tastes. But black soldiers carried this new musical style to Europe during World War I. Writer Lincoln Steffens said that after the war, "We found the whole world dancing to American jazz."[28]

The more energetic rhythms of all the new types of music led young people in the 1910s to abandon old-fashioned dances like the waltz for the fox-trot, turkey trot, horse trot, chicken scratch, lame duck, and grizzly bear. Collectively called "animal dances," the new steps shocked the older generation.

Sports

Spectator sports were very popular in the 1910s. One year, 1912, is typical of the decade:

The Boston Red Sox beat the New York Giants four games to three in the ninth World Series, which lasted eight games; called because of darkness, the second game was a tie and did not count. Harvard won all nine of its games to take the national college football championship and Joe Dawson captured the second Indianapolis 500 auto race, taking more than six hours to finish and averaging 78.72 miles per hour.

In Stockholm, Sweden, the United States collected twenty-three gold medals in the Olympic Games. Jim Thorpe, an Indian who attended Carlisle Indian School in Pennsylvania, won the Olympic pentathlon and decathlon to earn the title of world's greatest athlete and went on to star in professional football and baseball. Although Olympic officials stripped Thorpe of his medals when it was learned he had played semiprofessional baseball in 1909, they were later returned and in 1950 sportswriters named Thorpe "the greatest football player and male athlete of the first half of the Twentieth Century."[29]

Stars like Thorpe lured millions of sports fans to ballparks, racetracks, and football stadiums. The 1910s featured baseball greats like Ty Cobb, who played for twenty-four years and finished with a

These elegantly attired dancers, the women daringly showing their ankles, strut new steps to the latest jazz tunes. The new music and dance steps shocked older generations accustomed to such sedate dances as the waltz.

.367 average and a dozen batting titles, and Grover Cleveland Alexander, who in 1916 held opposing teams scoreless fifteen times and finished with ninety career shutouts and 3,503 strikeouts.

And then was George Herman "Babe" Ruth. The Babe began his career as a pitcher, winning twenty-three of twenty-five games in 1916 and three World Series games in 1917 for the Boston Red Sox. Ruth was such a powerful hitter that the Red Sox, needing his bat in the lineup every day, played him at first base or in the outfield on days he did not pitch. After slugging a major league record twenty-nine home runs in 1919 Ruth was traded to the New York Yankees, where he became a legendary home run king.

The heavyweight boxing champion from 1908 to 1915 was Jack Johnson, the first black to hold the title. White boxing fans reviled Johnson because of his race, his flamboyant lifestyle, and because he dated white women, a taboo at the time. Before the decade was over, however, boxing gained one of its most popular champions—Jack Dempsey, the "Manassa Mauler," who on July 4, 1919, knocked out defending champion Jess Willard, who had beaten Johnson.

In 1919 jockey Johnny Loftus rode Sir Barton to the first Triple Crown, winning the Kentucky Derby, Preakness, and Belmont Stakes races. That same year the Indianapolis 500 resumed after a two-year hiatus caused by the war and Howard Wilcox won with an average speed of 88.05 miles per hour—cars were slowly getting faster.

Football became so popular that colleges began building large stadiums; the first, in 1914, was the Yale Bowl, which seated eighty thousand. Eastern schools like Harvard and Yale dominated the sport but in 1913 midwestern upstart Notre Dame defeated Harvard 35-13. Professional football was of only minor interest to sports fans until 1921 when the National Football League began.

Reading

But the nation was not preoccupied solely with athletic pursuits. The decade saw a continued growth in reading for pleasure and information.

In 1918 the nation's 2,441 newspapers had a circulation of 33 million, more than twice the number of papers sold in 1900. The *New York Sunday World* in 1913 unveiled a unique new feature, the crossword puzzle. Created by editor Arthur Wynne, the *World* for the next decade was the nation's only newspaper to offer this intellectual challenge. Comic strips began appearing in the twentieth century; by 1910 *Mutt and Jeff, Happy Hooligan,* and the *Katzenjammer Kids* were important reasons to buy a newspaper.

While Willa Cather, Theodore Dreiser, and Jack London were writing novels that

Jack Johnson and the "Great White Hope"

The most hated athlete in America from 1908 to 1915 was heavyweight boxing champion Jack Johnson. He was hated mainly because he was black.

In 1908 Johnson defeated Canadian Tommy Burns in Australia to win the heavyweight title. Any other boxer would have been a hero throughout the nation. Instead most Americans could not bear the thought of a black champion and began their search for the "Great White Hope"—a white fighter who could defeat Johnson.

But Johnson, who topped six feet by several inches and weighed more than two hundred pounds, kept disappointing them by winning every fight. Finally, legendary former champion Jim Jeffries was lured out of retirement to fight Johnson for a purse of $101,000, a huge sum at the time.

The title bout was in Reno, Nevada, on July 4, 1910. In a story for the *New York Herald* Jack London, the world-famous author of *Call of the Wild,* reported Johnson's victory: "Once again has Johnson sent down to defeat the chosen representative of the white race, and this time the greatest of them all." After the fight Johnson's mother commented, "He said he'd *bring home the bacon,* and the honey boy has gone and done it." The expression has been in popular use ever since.

The victory made whites in New York so angry they rioted, killing a half-dozen blacks, and there were attacks and attempted lynchings in Philadelphia, Washington, Atlanta, and St. Louis. White America hated Johnson not only because he had won a coveted title but because of his lifestyle, which included dating white women. He was once jailed on charges of transporting a white woman across state lines for immoral purposes, though she was his friend and later became his wife.

Tired of the discrimination he faced in the United States, Johnson moved to Europe

Jack Johnson flashes the fighting stance that helped him become the first black heavyweight boxing champion.

for several years and was treated in London and Paris as the sports hero he really was. Johnson finally lost his title on April 5, 1915, in Havana, Cuba, to Jess Willard. Out of shape and past his prime at thirty-seven, Johnson lasted twenty-three rounds against a much larger, younger opponent.

would become classics, Robert Frost, Carl Sandburg, Vachel Lindsay, and Sherwood Anderson were penning some of the finest American poetry ever written.

Although it was a period in which many important writers were discovered, millions of readers looking for adventure fell in love with two new writers in particular. Zane Grey was on his way to becoming the most popular western novelist of all time with novels like *Riders of the Purple Sage* and Edgar Rice Burroughs began writing fantastic adventures like *Tarzan of the Apes*. Burroughs's jungle lord, one of the most popular fictional heroes of all time, was introduced in 1912. Lord Greystoke crossed over into the new medium of the movies only two years later in the first of his many screen appearances.

The first Tarzan novel appeared in *All-Story,* one of many magazines popular in the new century. They cost just a dime— the move in the 1890s to include paid advertising in magazines made them affordable—and by 1918 the nation's 1,230 weekly magazines had a circulation of 31.2 million, nearly double the number of readers of 1904.

The Automobile Changes America

The automobile entered the new century scorned as a rich man's toy, ridiculed by most as a noisy, smelly contraption that could never replace the horse. It exited the

Edgar Rice Burroughs, the creator of Tarzan, was one of the decade's most popular authors. Burroughs's legendary ape man was a hit in books and movies, remaining popular long after Burroughs died in 1950.

second decade as an indispensable part of American life.

In September 1892, William Morrison of Des Moines, Iowa, drove an electric-powered vehicle through the streets of Chicago, and police had to hold back curious onlookers who had no idea what the strange-looking vehicle was. At the same time brothers Charles and Frank Duryea of Springfield, Massachusetts, were testing their gasoline-powered car indoors—they were afraid people would laugh at them if they took it outside. But on September 21, 1893, they finally mustered the courage to drive it through their hometown.

America's love affair with cars, nick-named "horseless carriages," had a rocky beginning. Woodrow Wilson once said, "Nothing has spread socialistic feeling in this country more than the use of the automobile. To the countryman, they are a picture of the arrogance of wealth, with all its independence and carelessness." [30] Most Americans at the turn of the century viewed them suspiciously, like the newspaper editor who wrote that the automobile "is well-named the 'devil wagon.'" [31]

In 1900 fewer than eight thousand automobiles competed with 18 million horses and mules and 10 million bicycles used for transportation. The first cars were lightweight with high, solid rubber tires, one-cylinder engines, and bicycle chains to turn the wheels. They were expensive, had frequent mechanical problems, and seemed impractical because travel was so difficult.

The main obstacle to driving at the turn of the century was that there were less than ten miles of paved concrete in the entire nation. In 1903 it took eight days for thirty-four auto enthusiasts to drive from Pittsburgh to New York City, a journey easily made today in six hours, because of the lack of roads. In 1916 Congress passed a bill to finance road construction, which would help make auto travel easier.

Poor roads and balky machines, however, did not stop enthusiasts from motoring into the countryside for pleasure, the first great use of the new vehicle. In 1907

Independent magazine noted "the endless procession of automobiles firing out into the country" from New York City each weekend as testimony to "[the] hold the sport has taken upon the popular fancy." [32]

Henry Ford almost single-handedly made automobiles popular by manufacturing cars that were reliable, simple to operate, and affordable. In 1903 he opened his first factory in Detroit and in 1908 began producing the Model T. Ford called it his "universal car" because he wanted to standardize one model to cut costs while at the same time making it the best car possible. "The way to make automobiles," Ford said, "is to make one automobile just like another automobile, just as one match is like another match when it comes from the match factory." [33]

Ford's stroke of genius was to introduce the moving assembly line to manufacturing in 1913, a principle borrowed from meatpackers. Most companies employed versatile mechanics to assemble cars by hand in one spot, with parts brought to them. But on assembly lines workers would install a small part or perform a simple function as the auto was carried past them, which greatly speeded up production. By 1914 Ford was manufacturing 250,000 cars a year, nearly as many as all his competitors combined.

Increased efficiency and savings allowed Ford to keep cutting the price of the Model T. In 1909 Ford made 18,664 cars for $950 each; in 1919 he produced 533,707 cars

This scene from Bathing Beauties, *a Mack Sennett movie circa 1914, features an open air touring car.*

and sold them for $525. By 1925 a new Model T cost only $290 and by 1927 Ford had sold 15 million of the cars lovingly nicknamed "flivvers" (they shook so hard, the joke went, that they were good for your liver) and "tin lizzies."

In 1920 Americans were driving over 8 million passenger cars, more than the rest of the world combined. In just one generation automobiles had captured the hearts and minds of Americans.

Modern Technology

The second decade also saw the airplane, which had only gotten off the ground a few years earlier, soar to new heights. When the Wright brothers, Orville and Wilbur, made the first manned flight December 17, 1903, at Kitty Hawk, North Carolina, Orville only

remained aloft for twelve seconds and flew only 120 feet.

But within eight years an airplane was able to fly from coast to coast, though it took pilot Calbraith R. Rodgers nearly seven weeks to complete the trip. He took off from New York City in a biplane, an aircraft with a double set of wings, on September 12 and landed in Long Beach, California, November 5. The total flight time between stops to refuel and rest was 82 hours and 4 minutes.

Airplanes were still rather flimsy and undependable and few people were willing to be passengers, much less pay for the honor. But the U.S. military began looking at their possible use in warfare. On November 14, 1910, a biplane flown by Eugene Ely was the first to take off from the deck of a U.S. warship, the *Birmingham*. Airplanes proved to be a valuable new weapon in World War I.

Because of their speed airplanes were able to deliver mail faster than ever before, an important advance in an era of slow and erratic communications. Likewise, the first coast-to-coast telephone call was a significant step.

On January 25, 1915, Alexander Graham Bell, who invented the telephone, spoke from San Francisco to his assistant, Thomas A. Watson, in New York: "Mr. Watson, come here, I want you."[34] Bell had spoken the same words to Watson in 1876 when his telephone worked for the first time—only instead of being in a nearby room as in 1876 the two men were separated by several thousand miles.

In 1900 almost all of the more than 1 million telephones in operation were on local circuits. The circuit that carried the first transcontinental call included 3,400 miles of copper wire that weighed 5.9 million pounds, was strung on 130,000 poles, and cost over $2 million to build.

Another new form of communication was wireless communication, invented in 1894 by Guglielmo Marconi. By 1912 wireless was used for a variety of communication needs, including sending distress signals at sea. When the *Titanic* sank on the night of April 14, 1912, operators on the doomed liner were able to alert at least ten nearby ships, signaling aid for some seven hundred survivors.

The signal that went out from the *Titanic* was in Morse code but within a few years technology was developed to transmit voices by wireless, a form of communication that became known as radio. On April 30, 1915, wireless experimenters from the U.S. Navy communicated from Washington, D.C., to the Panama Canal Zone. On July 27, 1915, the navy also helped broadcast remarks from Theodore Vail, president of the American Telephone and Telegraph Company, from Washington, D.C., to a naval site in San Francisco.

Several hours later it was learned that another navy receiver in Honolulu also picked up the remarks.

In the summer of 1920 the nation's first radio station, WWJ in Detroit, went on the air to begin a whole new era in mass communication.

Boy Scouts, Lincoln Logs, and Mother's Day

Children benefited from some exciting developments in the 1910s. The Boy Scouts, a youth movement imported from England, began operating in America in 1910, giving boys new opportunities to explore the wild and learn new skills. The Campfire Girls, a counterpart organization, was also chartered that year.

In 1913 an advertisement proclaimed "Hello Boys! Make Lots of Toys!" The ad was for a brand-new toy called the Erector Set, which encouraged boys to make anything their imagination could conceive.

Lincoln Logs, a wooden building block set still popular at the end of the twentieth century, also made their appearance in this era. Lincoln Logs, named for Abraham Lincoln, whose boyhood home was a log cabin, were created by John L. Wright, son of famed architect Frank Lloyd Wright.

Mothers also got a treat in 1914 when Congress approved a resolution proclaiming the second Sunday in May as "Mother's Day." Every year since then mothers have been honored on this special day.

Chapter Four

Theodore Roosevelt, who commanded a group of soldiers known as the Rough Riders, leads the charge up San Juan Hill in Cuba during the Spanish-American War. As president, Roosevelt acted forcefully to bring the United States out of its isolationist shell and become a major world power.

Edging into World Affairs

In his 1796 farewell address President George Washington warned the nation he helped found to "steer clear of permanent alliances"[35] with other countries. It was a piece of advice Americans took to heart and resolutely followed for the next hundred years.

Isolated geographically by the Atlantic and Pacific Oceans, Americans felt free to ignore the world as they went about fulfilling their goal of manifest destiny—the belief in their divine right to push westward three thousand miles and inhabit the vast expanse between the original thirteen colonies and the Pacific Ocean. By 1890 the United States had succeeded in stretching its borders to the Pacific Ocean and in 1912 Arizona and New Mexico became the forty-seventh and forty-eighth states.

Americans now began looking beyond their shores but were uncertain what role they should take in world affairs. Theodore Roosevelt felt he had the answer to that vital twentieth-century question:

In foreign affairs we must make up our minds that, whether we wish it or not, we are a great people and must play a great part in the world. It is not open to us to choose whether we will play that great part or not. We have to play it. All we can decide is whether we shall play it well or ill.[36]

New American Possessions

The last decades of the nineteenth century have been called the age of imperialism because European nations were aggressively conquering territory and creating colonies in Africa, China, Southeast Asia, and the South Pacific. Imperialism is the control or acquisition of one nation for the economic or political gain of another, usually through military force. Belgium, France, Great Britain, Germany, Italy, Portugal, and Spain all overpowered weaker nations to expand and reinforce their own power; the interests of the peoples they subjugated were of little concern.

European nations rationalized imperialist policies through a belief in white, Anglo-Saxon superiority. Imperialists claimed it was their duty to bring civilized culture and ideas to races and ethnic groups they considered inferior. This attitude, popularly known as "the white man's burden" from a poem by English author Rudyard Kipling, was shared by many Americans.

In his popular 1885 book *Our Country*, Congregationalist minister Josiah Strong wrote that "God, with infinite wisdom and skill, is training the Anglo-Saxon race" to spread "the largest liberty, the purest Christianity, the highest civilization . . . over the

This patriotic magazine cover reflects America's awakening interest in world affairs. The "call to arms" sounded by the bugler is symbolic of the nation's desire to join other nations in the drive to gain new possessions, such as those it won in the Spanish-American War like the Philippine Islands.

earth." He predicted this higher type of civilization would move down "upon Mexico, down upon Central and South America, out upon the islands of the seas, over upon Africa and beyond." [37]

It was during this period that the United States joined the race to acquire territory and power. The spoils of its victory over Spain in the Spanish-American War in 1898 included not only nearby Cuba and Puerto Rico but the Philippine Islands and the island of Guam, which were six thousand miles away.

At the end of the war the United States retained the former Spanish possessions as colonies instead of granting independence, although its stated goal in the conflict was to free Cubans from Spanish rule. Cuba remained a U.S. protectorate until 1934, the Philippines were not freed until after World War II in 1946, and Puerto Rico and Guam became U.S. territories.

After the Spanish-American War there was a great debate on whether to retain control of the Philippines. In a 1900 speech to those backing expansion President William McKinley explained why he recommended annexation of the Philippines:

The truth is I didn't want the Philippines and when they came to us as a gift from the gods, I did not know what to do about them. And then one night it came to me this way—(1) that we could not give them back to Spain—that would be cowardly and dishonorable;

(2) that we could not turn them over to France or Germany—our commercial rivals in the Orient; (3) that we could not leave them to themselves—they were unfit for self-government—and they would soon have anarchy and misrule over there worse than Spain's was; and (4) that there was nothing left for us to do but to take them all, and to educate the Filipinos, and uplift and civilize and Christianize them. [38]

The decision to retain the Philippine Islands proved costly for the United States. In the three years after the Spanish-American War seventy thousand U.S. soldiers battled Philippine rebels who demanded freedom for their country. In the brutal war to subdue the rebels five thousand Americans, twenty-five thousand rebel soldiers, and two hundred thousand civilians died.

If the Philippines came to the United States as "a gift," annexation of the Hawaiian islands was pure theft. The United States acquired the South Pacific islands of Hawaii in a blatant act of American imperialism in 1893. American businessmen organized a revolution to overthrow Queen Liliuokalani, an illegal takeover aided by armed U.S. Marines. Hawaii was formally annexed as a U.S. territory five years later after the Spanish-American War showed it was needed as a military outpost to protect growing American interests in the South Pacific and Far East.

America Awakens

Although Hawaii's main value was as a harbor for U.S. military ships, the decision to annex the islands was linked directly to economic considerations. A new and important factor in formulating foreign policy in the twentieth century was the necessity for America, the world's leading industrial nation, to develop free and open markets for its products.

"American factories," Indiana senator Albert Beveridge bragged in 1898, "are making more than the American people can use; American soil is producing more than they can consume. Fate has written our policy for us: the trade of the world must and shall be ours."[39] Hawaii, located midway between the United States and the Far East, gave America a military base from which to influence events in the Far East and insure that European nations would not cut off America from economic opportunities there.

Maintaining U.S. rights to free and open trade motivated the United States in 1900 to successfully demand a so-called open door policy in China. Until then France, Germany, Great Britain, Japan, and Russia had been seizing territory in China, which was too weak to fight back.

Hawaii

"The Hawaiian pear is now fully ripe and this is the golden hour for the United States to pluck it." That was the message U.S. diplomats in Hawaii relayed to Washington in 1893. That was the way Hawaii became the nation's fiftieth state, by being "plucked" from Queen Liliuokalani and the people she ruled.

American ships involved in whaling and trade with China began stopping at the Hawaiian Islands at the end of the eighteenth century and religious missionaries and other Americans began arriving in the 1820s. Though the Hawaiian Islands were more than three thousand miles west of California, they soon became important to America because of their lucrative sugar crop and other economic interests.

American businessmen became alarmed when Queen Liliuokalani succeeded her brother, King David Kalakaua, when he died in 1891. A determined nationalist who wanted Hawaiians to rule the islands, Liliuokalani was less cooperative with foreign businessmen. So in 1893 Sanford B. Dole and other American businessmen established a revolutionary "committee of safety" to overthrow the Hawaiian monarchy. Hawaii's fate was sealed when Dole gained the support of John L. Stevens, the U.S. minister to Hawaii.

On January 16, 1893, when the committee engineered the queen's overthrow, Stevens ordered ashore 150 U.S. Marines from the cruiser *Boston* "to protect American lives and property in case of riot." There was no threat to any U.S. businesses or citizens but the marines helped stop any resistance to the illegal takeover and imprisoned Queen Liliuokalani in her palace.

Stevens immediately granted recognition to the provisional government set up by Americans, but President Grover Cleveland believed Queen Liliuokalani had been illegally overthrown and refused to annex Hawaii. Congress debated the matter for several years and did not approve annexation until the Spanish-American War began, when Hawaii's military value as a naval base became important. Hawaii was annexed as a territory in 1898 and in 1959 became the fiftieth state.

Because America feared it would be shut out of the China trade and other opportunities in the Far East it pressured its rivals to cease taking Chinese land and to keep the country open to all diplomatic and trading partners.

In 1904 President Roosevelt also acted to protect American interests in the Far East by mediating an end to the war between Russia and Japan over control of territories in Manchuria and Korea. He won the Nobel Peace Prize for his efforts.

Latin America

Closer to home, America now decided it needed to wield more power over Latin America and the Caribbean to protect its interests. The United States had considered Latin American nations under its sphere of influence since 1823 when President James Monroe warned European nations not to interfere in the Western Hemisphere. One of President Roosevelt's favorite phrases was an African proverb: "Speak softly and carry a big stick, you will go far."[40] In 1904 he used the "big stick" of American military and economic power to take the Monroe Doctrine one step further.

In Roosevelt's corollary to the Monroe Doctrine, he proclaimed that the United States had the right to exercise international police powers in Western Hemisphere nations if they failed to meet their financial obligations to other countries. Roosevelt was worried that if they failed to pay their debts, European countries

would seize them. In 1902, for instance, Germany and Great Britain took control of several ports in Venezuela to force the country to pay some overdue debts.

This brash new policy resulted in a series of U.S. interventions in the next two decades to protect American investments in the Caribbean and Central America. In 1904, when a revolt broke out in the Dominican Republic, European nations began demanding payment of $40 million in defaulted loans. To keep out Europeans the United States intervened militarily in the republic, took over the collection of customs taxes, and used the money to repay the loans. In 1906 the United States sent troops to both Guatemala and Nicaragua, countries in which American bankers controlled nearly 50 percent of all trade.

Several more interventions occurred in the next few years: Cuba in 1906, Honduras in 1907, Nicaragua again in 1909. The interventions were all prompted by political instability and financial problems that threatened American investments in railroads, mines, and sugar, banana, and coffee plantations.

Another vital U.S. asset Roosevelt wanted to protect was the Panama Canal, which the United States began building in 1906 and finished in 1914. The canal was important because it cut eight thousand miles from the sea journey between America's east and west coasts, making the United States more powerful economically and militarily by shortening the time to move ships from one side of the continent to another.

The way the United States managed to secure rights to Panama also involved intervention by American forces. In 1903 the United States had offered Colombia a payment of $10 million and $250,000 a year rent for the right to build the canal across a six-mile-wide strip of land in Panama, a province of Colombia. When Colombia demanded millions of dollars more, the two nations were unable to come to an agreement. This infuriated the impatient, volatile Roosevelt, who wanted

the canal built as soon as possible, partly to help his chances for reelection in 1904.

Panamanian nationalists had campaigned for freedom from Colombia for many years but all previous attempts at revolution had been smashed by the Colombian army. When they revolted again in November 1903, Roosevelt saw his chance to secure a canal route for the United States. He ordered a warship to Panama that prevented Colombian forces from landing and quelling the armed revolution. When Roosevelt quickly recognized the new government in Panama,

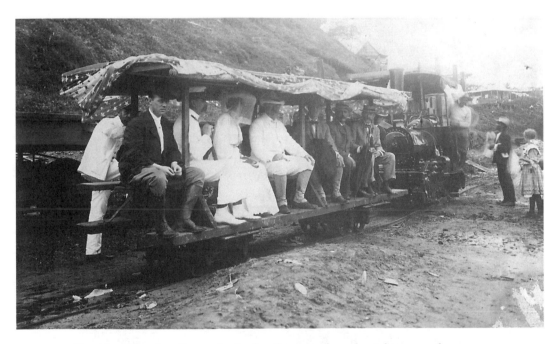

President Theodore Roosevelt, the fourth person from the right among those seated on a railroad car, visits the future site of the Panama Canal. The opening of the canal in 1914 strengthened the United States economically and militarily by enabling ships to travel much faster between its two coasts.

A dredging ship leaves the east chamber of the Pedro Miguel Locks on October 24, 1913, to continue work on deepening the Panama Canal. Construction of the canal was one of the most complex engineering tasks of the early twentieth century.

the grateful new country agreed to a treaty that granted the United States land for a canal zone.

Dollar and Missionary Diplomacy

Roosevelt's policies had been based in part on using the nation's economic power to influence other countries and his successor, William Taft, built on this philosophy to create "dollar diplomacy." Taft urged U.S. businesses to lend money directly to Nicaragua to help the struggling nation, to increase investments in Cuba and other Latin American countries, and to take part in an international syndicate trying to finance railroads in Manchuria, a country that bordered China.

But the policy did not work very well. In 1912 another revolution in Nicaragua again prompted U.S. intervention with two thousand marines. U.S. forces occupied Nicaragua until 1933 to protect American investments.

Although Woodrow Wilson had promised to reject "dollar diplomacy," as president he continued to act as Taft had to preserve American interests. In 1914 he ordered U.S. troops into Haiti to protect American lives and property after yet another violent revolution, and they remained there for twenty years. The United States also intervened again in 1916 in the Dominican Republic, where U.S. troops stayed until 1934.

Wilson's justification was different from Taft's, however, and his Latin American policy came to be called "missionary diplomacy." Like the imperialists who believed in the "white man's burden," Wilson felt it was America's duty to teach other nations democratic principles of government. He also wanted the United States to pursue new possessions in the Caribbean and Far East as "an engine of liberty" [41] to further spread democracy. Wilson purchased the Virgin Islands from Denmark in 1917 under this new philosophy.

Intervention in Mexico

Upset by what seemed an endless round of revolutions and unrest in Latin America, Wilson once told a British diplomat, "I am going to teach the South American republics to elect good men!" [42] However, Wilson's missionary zeal almost caused a war between the United States and Mexico. And the mistakes Wilson made in dealing with its largest neighbor to the south showed how naive the United States still was concerning foreign policy issues.

In 1913 Wilson refused to recognize Victoriano Huerta, the new Mexican leader who had overthrown the government and killed former president Francisco Madero. Madero was elected in 1911 as part of a liberal coalition that had ousted dictator Porfirio Díaz in 1910. Wilson was angry because he favored Madero, who was trying to reform Mexico's economy and create a democratic government.

Because most nations quickly recognized Huerta, Wilson's refusal caused tensions between the two nations. In April 1914 when they put into the port of Tampico, a group of U.S. sailors were harassed by Mexican authorities and briefly detained by officials. It was a minor incident. But when Huerta refused to issue a formal apology for the Tampico incident, Wilson retaliated for the alleged show of disrespect for America by blockading the port city of Veracruz. His real reason, however, was to stop a shipment of German arms from being delivered to Huerta. Wilson later ordered U.S. Marines to seize Veracruz; 19 Americans and 126 Mexicans were killed in the subsequent fight.

For several weeks war appeared imminent but Argentina, Brazil, and Chile, known as the ABC powers, stepped in to mediate the dispute. In July, when Wilson still refused to support a government that had come to power by force, Huerta, who was not very popular in Mexico, stepped down and fled to exile in Spain.

The new leader was General Venustiano Carranza. But Wilson again decided not to accept the new government and instead backed Francisco "Pancho" Villa, one of Huerta's generals, who had pledged cooperation with the United States. But Wilson had made another big mistake. Villa, more opportunistic bandit than revolutionary, had little support and Carranza easily defeated him.

In October 1915 Wilson finally relented and recognized the Carranza government after it promised not to confiscate foreign-owned property and to protect the lives of foreigners. This was important to Wilson because U.S. businesses had more than $1 billion in investments in Mexico and more than forty thousand Americans lived there.

But Wilson's problems were still not over. In January 1916 Villa and his followers stopped a train in northern Mexico and killed sixteen American passengers. Two months later they raided Columbus, New Mexico, and killed nineteen more people. Villa, who was trying to get the United States to intervene in Mexico to weaken Carranza, succeeded by making Wilson angry enough to send a punitive expedition after him.

U.S. forces led by General John J. Pershing roared across the border in pursuit of

Pancho Villa, who was more bandit than revolutionary, took U.S. troops on a chase through Mexico for several months in 1916 after several deadly assaults on American towns near the border with Mexico.

Villa. Although Pershing never caught up with the wily and elusive Villa, his troops had several clashes with Mexican troops who resented the intrusion of U.S. troops. War once again seemed inevitable but early in 1917 Wilson recalled Pershing to end the futile eleven-month escapade.

The U.S. military now had a more pressing problem to deal with—America was edging closer every day to declaring war on Germany.

World War I—A Surprise to America

The outbreak of World War I in Europe in August 1914 surprised most Americans: One congressman said war came "like lightning out of a clear blue sky."[43] Surprised but not particularly threatened, most Americans felt the conflict was so far away it could not affect the United States.

Like nearly everyone else in the United States, Wilson felt America should stay out of the war. On August 19 the president asked citizens to "be impartial in thought as well as in action" and declared the United States would be "neutral in fact as well as in name." Several weeks later Wilson designated October 4 as Peace Sunday and asked Americans to go to church and "unite their petitions to Almighty God that . . . He vouchsafe his children healing peace and restore once

General John J. Pershing at U.S. headquarters in Mexico. Although Pershing failed in his mission to capture Pancho Villa, he went on to glory as commander of U.S. forces in World War I.

more concord among men and nations." On October 5 the *New York Times* headline read: "Whole Nation Prays for Peace."[44]

However, Wilson and the rest of the nation would soon learn that neither prayers nor promises of neutrality could keep the United States out of the first global conflict in history.

Chapter Five

U.S. Marines wave a jaunty good-bye as their troop train pulls out of camp, the first leg of their journey to France to fight in World War I. The horrors of the battlefield, however, would soon change their naive belief that war was a grand adventure.

The United States Goes to War

At first even President Woodrow Wilson did not believe World War I would have any serious effect on America. "He looked upon the war as a distant event, terrible and tragic, but one which did not concern us closely in the political sense,"[45] his trusted aide Colonel Edward M. House wrote years later.

War, however, did not surprise Wilson. In the spring of 1914 he sent Colonel House ("colonel" was an honorary title used by many southerners) to Europe to investigate reports of escalating tensions among various nations. With foresight verging on clairvoyance, House had written Wilson that "the whole of Germany is charged with electricity. Everybody's nerves are tense. It only requires a spark to set the whole thing off."[46]

That spark came in a city few Americans had ever heard of—Sarajevo.

The Roots of World War I

On June 28, 1914, Archduke Franz Ferdinand, the heir to the throne of the Austro-Hungarian Empire, and his wife, Sophie, were shot to death in Sarajevo, the capital of Bosnia. The assassin was Gavrilo Princip, a nationalist from neighboring Serbia who wanted Bosnian Serbs freed from rule by Austria-Hungary.

As the archduke's automobile rolled through Sarajevo in a joyous royal procession, Princip jumped on the running board of the open car and shot the royal couple. A little more than a month later, on August 4, Germany, an ally of Austria-Hungary, sent its army marching into Belgium to begin the bloodiest conflict the world had ever known.

Americans found it hard to believe that the death of a little-known member of European royalty could cause a war. However, the archduke's death merely ignited a multitude of smoldering resentments and hatreds stemming from Europe's contentious past and the current colonial aspirations of the nations that went to war.

The countries that fought in the Great War, as it was named, were divided into the Allies (France, Great Britain, Belgium, and Russia) and the Central Powers (Germany and Austria-Hungary) but as the war continued many other nations also fought. The Ottoman Empire (Turkey) and Bulgaria sided with the Central Powers while two dozen nations joined the Allies, including Italy, Japan, China, and even a few tiny Latin American countries.

The speed with which nations went to war was a function of alliances and secret pacts between European countries. As rivalries had become more bitter near the end of the nineteenth century, various nations had

German soldiers wearing their trademark spiked helmets man their fortifications, part of the hundreds of miles of trenches in which soldiers from both sides lived, fought, and died during World War I.

promised to fight together if either was attacked. One pact was between Germany and the Austro-Hungarian Empire, a vast land that included Austria, Hungary, Czechoslovakia, Bosnia, and Serbia. When Austria-Hungary declared war on Serbia the day after the assassination, Germany quickly followed suit. France, Great Britain, and Russia then joined forces with Serbia.

In the month after the archduke was killed there were opportunities for the na-

tions to back away from their pledges to fight. But most historians feel Germany was looking for an excuse for war so it could expand its territory. Germany, the leader of the Central Powers, rejected peace overtures and touched off the war by sending its armies through Belgium to attack France, an old foe in many conflicts.

Thus began a war that in five years would consume the lives of 8.5 million soldiers and 22 million civilians, lead to the fall of several empires, create new na-

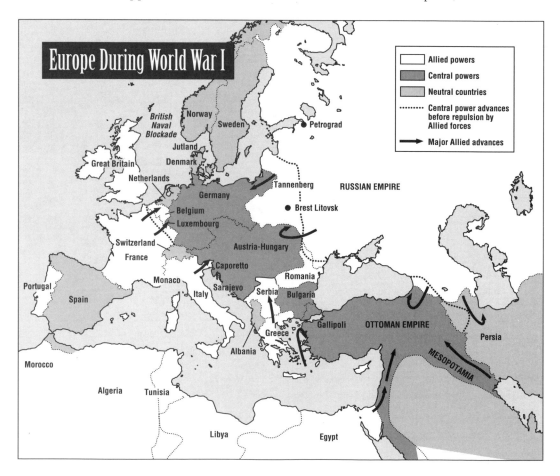

tions, and make the United States the savior of Europe.

The War Divides America

When war began, Americans were united in their desire to stay out of a conflict they saw as foolish and destructive. But as the fighting continued the nation was divided in many ways, especially over the issue of U.S. participation.

Many Americans of foreign birth supported their former homelands, raising war funds and trying to persuade their American friends and neighbors that their native country was in the right. The 1910 census shows that 8 million U.S. residents were from Germany or Austria-Hungary and 4.5 million from Ireland. Most of these immigrants supported the Central Powers; the Irish because they hated their English rulers. But nearly one-half of Americans could trace their ancestry to British or Canadian sources and millions more to Russia and France, and Americans as a whole had an abiding respect and love for the nation's English heritage.

Thousands of immigrants returned home to fight for their former countries and some U.S. citizens, either through sheer love of adventure or because they felt it was the right thing to do, enlisted in foreign armies. The Lafayette Escadrille, part of the French air corps, was made up of Americans.

The pacifist movement worked hard to keep the United States out of the war, led

American women were at the forefront of the drive to keep the United States out of World War I. Their opposition was summed up by the song "I Didn't Raise My Boy to Be a Soldier."

mostly by women like Jane Addams, the social worker who founded Hull House in Chicago. In 1915 Addams was elected president of the Women's Peace Party. She also headed the International Congress of Women, which met April 1915 in The Hague, Netherlands, to plead with European nations to quit fighting.

Newspapers generally backed U.S. participation and bitterly attacked dissenters.

Harshly criticized after the peace conference in the Netherlands, Addams claimed newspapers were trying "to make pacifist activity or propaganda seem so absurd that it would be absolutely without influence and its authors so discredited that nothing they might say or do would be regarded as worthy of attention."[47]

The Women's Peace Party, American Union Against Militarism, and New York's American Neutrality Conference Committee led marches and rallies in every major city. The League to Limit Armaments was formed in 1914 to counteract what it called the "outcry from jingoists and militarists" that the United States build up its military and go to war.

However, a growing group of Americans wanted the nation to fight or, at the very least, become stronger militarily so it could defend itself. The so-called preparedness movement was led by former president Theodore Roosevelt and groups like the National Defense League.

Easing Away from Neutrality

Though the United States had declared itself neutral, historians believe many Americans favored the Allied cause from the beginning. The German decision to invade neutral Belgium to gain an easy route to attack France was successful militarily but enraged Americans. In the January 7, 1915, issue of *Life* magazine editor Edward S. Martin said Belgium was "the great clear issue of this war."

He called Belgium "a martyr to civilization, sister to all who love liberty or law; assailed, polluted, trampled in the mire, heel marked in her breast, tattered, homeless."[48]

Pro-Allied sentiment started at the top with President Wilson. When Great Britain used its superior naval power to blockade European ports, resulting in the illegal seizure of U.S. goods bound for Central Power nations, Wilson only weakly protested the denial of U.S. supplies to Germany and its allies.

President Woodrow Wilson marches in a Preparedness Day parade. Although President Wilson initially opposed U.S. participation in World War I, he did more than any other U.S. official to help the Allies early in the conflict and to eventually join the fighting.

The United States also failed to remain neutral economically. Between 1914 and 1916 trade between the United States and Central Powers declined from $169 million to just over $1 million while trade with the Allies increased from $825 million to over $3 billion. Also during this period of alleged U.S. neutrality, Wall Street firms issued loans totaling $2.3 billion to the Allies but only $27 million to Germany.

The loans enabled the Allies to continue buying armaments, food, and other supplies from the United States, brought the U.S. economy out of a mild recession, and bound the nation ever more tightly to the Allies. "War was producing in the United States its own intoxication. People felt happy because they were busy and seemed to be making money. . . . Naturally, as the Allies were our customers, they became our friends,"[49] wrote newspaper editor William Allen White.

Submarine Warfare

Because the English navy ruled the seas, Germany decided to use submarines to stop the flow of U.S. supplies. German U-boats (*Unterseeboot* is the German word for submarine) began sinking commercial ships bound for Allied ports, firing on them without warning.

The crew of a German submarine lurks under the sea near the British Isles, searching for a target. During the war sneak attacks by U-boats devastated shipping between the United States and Great Britain.

On May 7, 1915, a submarine just off the coast of Ireland attacked the luxury liner *Lusitania*, which had left New York six days earlier. The passenger ship quickly sank after a single torpedo hit and 1,198 people died. The victims included 128 Americans, many of them women and children. Americans were horrified by an act perceived as deliberate murder, and many wanted the United States to go to war.

Wilson reacted cautiously. His official protest called for the Germans to promise to

The Sinking of the *Lusitania*

The *Lusitania* was one of the great "floating palaces" of its day, a luxury liner on which passengers crossed the Atlantic Ocean in style and comfort. Its 1,924 passengers and crew when it left New York on May 1, 1915, blithely ignored the threat of German submarines. Passengers even hung a sign that said: "To Hell with the Kaiser and His U-Boats." What they did not know was that the *Lusitania* was secretly carrying munitions for the Allies and the Germans had selected it as a target.

Six days later *Unterseeboot* (U-boat) 20 was lying submerged off the coast of Ireland. As Leutnant-Kapitan (Lieutenant Captain) Karl Schwieger looked through his periscope, the 755-foot-long, thirty-thousand-ton *Lusitania* came into view. He fired one torpedo, which struck with devastating force and sank the ship in only twenty minutes, killing 1,198 aboard, including 114 Americans and at least 63 infants. It is believed the torpedo hit the stored munitions, which caused an even greater explosion.

Robert Rankin of Washington, D.C., was on deck when the torpedo struck. "We saw what looked like a whale or a porpoise rising about three-quarters of a mile to starboard," he said. "We all knew what it was, but no one named it. . . . The explosion came clear up through the upper deck and pieces of the wreckage fell clean aft of where we were standing."

Schwieger had quite a different view through his periscope. "She has the appearance of being about to capsize," he wrote in his military log. "Great confusion on board. Life-boats being cleared and lowered to water. Many boats crowded, coming down bow first or stern first in the water and immediately fill and sink. The ship blows off. It appears as if the vessel will be afloat only a short time. I submerge to 24 meters and go to sea. I could not have fired a second torpedo into this throng of humanity attempting to save themselves."

warn ships before they attacked so passengers could escape, but Germany continued unrestricted submarine warfare until the sinking of the British ship *Sussex* on March 24, 1916. President Wilson warned Germany that he would sever diplomatic relations unless it quit unrestricted warfare. Germany, to keep America out of the war, agreed to warn ships before attacking.

The so-called Sussex Pledge temporarily defused the issue but the damage to Germany had already been done: Americans viewed the submarine as an evil, cowardly weapon and began to turn even more against the Central Powers.

The Election of 1916

Divisive emotions concerning the war intensified in 1916, a presidential election year. Roosevelt, who hated Wilson, attacked the president for being too timid to stand up for American rights, especially after the sinking of the *Lusitania*.

Wilson, however, had gradually become a convert to preparedness. He moved to increase the size of the small, weak U.S. Army and in 1915 approved establishment of the Citizens Military Training Corps, which would provide military training to 750,000 volunteers a year. He also helped win appropriations of more than $500 million to strengthen the army and navy.

The Democratic slogan for Wilson's re-election campaign was "He Kept Us Out of War!" Even Wilson realized how foolish that statement was. "I can't keep the country out of war," he complained to an aide in 1916. "They talk of me as though I were a god. Any little German lieutenant can put us into war at any time by some calculated outrage."[50]

In a very close election, Wilson managed to defeat Republican candidate Charles Evans Hughes, a Supreme Court justice. He captured 277 electoral votes to 254 for Hughes while winning the popular vote 9.1 million to 8.5 million.

America Is Pushed into War

On January 22, 1917, Wilson appealed to the Allies and Central Powers to quit fighting and forge a "peace without victory."[51] His plea fell on deaf ears, however, and the man who had kept the nation out of war would soon lead it into battle because of a series of events beyond his control.

On January 31 Germany renounced the Sussex Pledge and resumed unrestricted submarine warfare. The British blockade had been so successful that Germany was running short of food (it is estimated that during the war 750,000 Germans starved to death) and gambled the United States would not go to war over the decision. But on February 3, a German submarine sank the SS *Housatonic*, and Wilson severed diplomatic relations with Germany.

American war sentiment also gained strength on March 1 when U.S. officials released a volatile secret message that German foreign minister Arthur Zimmermann had sent to the German ambassador in Mexico. The note, intercepted by the British, told the ambassador that if the United States declared war on Germany he was to ask Mexico to help Germany fight the United States. In return Germany promised to help Mexico win back territory the United States had taken from it in Arizona, New Mexico, and Texas. The proposal outraged the nation.

The final straw came March 16 when three U.S. ships—*City of Memphis, Illinois,* and *Vigilancia*—were sunk by submarines. Five days later Wilson called a special session of Congress to declare war.

"There is only one choice we cannot make, we are incapable of making: We will not choose the path of submission," Wilson told Congress April 2. "We accept this challenge of hostile purposes. . . . The world must be made safe for democracy. God helping her, she can do no other [than fight]."[52]

Four days later Congress overwhelmingly agreed. In the House only fifty Democrats, thirty-two Republicans, a Socialist, and an Independent voted against war; all but five senators voted to declare war.

Patriotic young men crowd the decks of a U.S. battleship to sign up for naval duty during World War I. Although many Americans enlisted in the armed forces when their nation went to war, the federal government had to draft sailors and soldiers to raise an army large enough to help win the war.

Like most Americans, legislators were finally ready to go "Over There," as the popular song said, and teach Germany a lesson it would never forget.

Gearing Up for War

When the United States went to war the patriotic young men who enlisted in the army and navy felt they would be the ones who would "lick the Germans." But Wilson knew better. "It's not an army we must train, it is a nation,"[53] he said.

Wilson knew the United States had to do more than produce vast quantities of rifles, ships, and ammunition and mobilize millions of soldiers. Because the president knew U.S. participation would affect the daily lives of all Americans, he understood the need to unite everyone solidly behind the war effort. The result was the largest propaganda machine the nation had ever known.

The job of the Committee on Public Information (CPI) was to convince Americans that the decision to declare war was right and to secure their cooperation in achieving victory. Because for three years Americans had tried to steer clear of war, that was no easy task. Even when the United States entered the war Wilson referred to his country as an "associate power" of the Allied forces and not a full-fledged ally, a distinction that perhaps only Wilson could discern.

George Creel, a Progressive journalist who headed CPI, called his task "the world's greatest adventure in advertising." Creel said his goal was to turn Americans into a "white-hot mass . . . with fraternity, devotion, courage, and deathless determination"[54] to win the war.

Creel's agency provided newspapers with up to six pounds of daily news releases and organized a small army of seventy-five thousand speakers called "Four Minute Men" who spread out across the nation to rally citizens with more than 7.5 million patriotic pep talks. CPI also wrote and distributed 60 million patriotic pamphlets, booklets, and leaflets, many in German,

A World War I recruiting poster urges young men to join the Tank Corps. The devilish looking animal attacking the tanks represents German soldiers who are the enemy. War propaganda attempted to make Americans think of enemy soldiers as beasts instead of human beings.

Italian, Russian, and other languages so immigrants could read them. It also plastered the nation with colorful patriotic posters and helped the fledgling motion picture industry make prowar movies. The agency also distributed propaganda to other nations to convince them America was doing the right thing.

Mobilizing for War

Following the declaration of war Congress granted Wilson unprecedented broad powers that made him the most powerful president the nation had ever known. He was given virtual control over the economy and authority to create new agencies and enact new laws to win the war.

Wilson's first task was to build up the military. When the war began the United States had only about two hundred thousand soldiers in the army and several thousand in the navy. When only thirty-two thousand men enlisted in the first few weeks after war was declared, Wilson realized the nation needed to draft soldiers. But some congressmen resisted his proposal for the Selective Service System because they feared a repeat of the draft riots and desertions that occurred during the Civil War. Senator James Reed of Missouri predicted the "streets of our American cities will be running with blood on registration day."[55]

But on June 5, when every American male age twenty-one to thirty-one was ordered to register with the new Selective

Service System, 10 million men voluntarily and peaceably signed up. The draft age was later expanded in two registrations in 1918; altogether more than 24 million men registered.

Before the war was over more than 4 million men served in the military and more than 2 million went overseas to fight. However, the first draftees did not report for training until September 17 and it was

Draft Lottery

Secretary of War Newton Baker quoted in volume 5 of *Our Times* said the United States was forced to resort to a military draft to raise an army for one very simple reason: "By 1917 the glory had passed from war. Young men saw soldiering as cruel duty rather than as sport."

Realizing that draft procedures during the Civil War had sparked riots and angered many Americans, the federal government tried to make the draft as fair as possible. The first step was to have every male register with the new Selective Service System on June 5, 1917, in their local voting precincts, a spot picked to make the act appear as patriotic and innocent as casting a ballot.

Blindfolded, Secretary of War Newton Baker draws the first number in the draft lottery for World War I from a goldfish bowl.

Ten million men between the ages of twenty-one and thirty-one registered, and the government decided the first wave of draftees would number 687,000. The question now was, What is a fair way to pick draftees out of all the men who registered? The government decided on a lottery system based on the numbers local draft boards had assigned to each registrant. There were 4,500 local draft boards, the largest of which had registered 10,500 men.

So in Washington on July 20 a large glass bowl was filled with 10,500 black cap-

sules containing numbered slips. Baker drew out the first slip—it was number 258. That meant that every man who had registered for the draft at a local board and had been given the number 258 was drafted. Officials drew numbers from 9:49 A.M. until 2 A.M. the next morning.

The numbers were relayed around the nation by telephone and telegraph and posted at local draft offices, where crowds were waiting to hear the news. A letter soon followed that told the draftee when to report for active duty.

not until 1918 that significant numbers of the American Expeditionary Force (AEF) landed in France.

A War of Smokestacks

The next task, even more difficult, was to mobilize the nation's economy. In 1917 Secretary of War Newton D. Baker said, "War is no longer Samson with his shield and spear and sword, and David with his sling. It is the conflict of smokestacks now, the combat of the driving wheel and the engine." [56]

Wilson relied on his wartime powers to reshape the nation's economy so it could produce the weapons and supplies the war demanded. He created agencies such as the War Industries Board, Food Administration, Fuel Administration, and National War Labor Board to control various segments of the economy. The government also took control of the railroads, which were vital for transportation, and the shipbuilding industry. New ships were desperately needed to ferry supplies to Europe because German submarines had successfully sunk so many.

The War Industries Board, the most powerful new agency, was headed by Wall Street broker Bernard Baruch. It had dictatorial power to allocate raw material such as steel, fix prices, and coordinate American and Allied purchases.

At first many business executives balked at this unprecedented government control of business. But when Horace Dodge and Henry Ford resisted orders to quit making cars and start producing war products, Baruch threatened to cut off rail service to their factories. Because they could not produce any products without deliveries of supplies they soon fell in line with federal demands.

The government also won the support of industries by allowing them to profit on the military contracts it issued. In fact, so many people made so much money that the public invented the term "war millionaires" for businessmen who earned that status because of the conflict.

American industry was slow to retool for the production of matériel, however, which meant many war industries did not reach peak production until the end of the war. U.S. factories manufactured only 64 tanks, and many ships for which plans were completed were not built until the fighting had ended, though on July 4, 1918, 100 new vessels were launched simultaneously in honor of the nation's birthday. In 1917 factories turned out 2,148 airplanes and the next year more than 14,000, but most did not fly into combat because it took so long to ship them overseas.

Another pressing need was for food, not only for the AEF but for Allied armies and millions of starving civilians in countries ravaged by the war. The Food Administration, headed by future president Herbert Hoover, asked U.S. farmers to increase their production. The government secured their cooperation by setting high prices for wheat ($2.20 a bushel) and other farm products.

Americans did their part by conserving food and growing vegetables at home in "victory gardens." The result was that the United States was able to triple its prewar shipments of wheat, sugar, meat, and fat to the Allies.

Paying for the War

Financing the war was another problem. By 1917 the treasuries of England and the other Allies were nearly depleted, and Allied governments turned to the United States for loans even as it worked to raise and equip its own army. The war cost the United States about $33 billion including about $7 billion in loans to Allied nations. The federal government raised taxes to collect some $10.5 billion but nearly two-thirds of the funding, or $23 billion, came from people who bought Liberty and Victory savings bonds and stamps.

Income tax rates, which ranged from 1 to 7 percent before the war, now ranged from 4 to an astounding 70.3 percent, the highest bracket reserved for people with incomes of more than $1 million. It was a tax burden that fell heavily on the rich, with those making less than $3,000 in 1918 contributing less than 4 percent of all receipts.

Americans gladly purchased bonds and saving certificates. Coins used to buy bonds or stamps were called "silver bullets" to beat the Germans and slogans like "Give Until It Hurts" and "Lick a Stamp and Lick the Kaiser" made buying them seem patriotic. Movie star Douglas Fairbanks and other celebrities helped raise money by drawing tens of thousands of people to war bond rallies. On average during the war each adult American lent the government $400.

This poster combines the American flag, a pretty girl, and sailors manning a large gun in a vivid attempt to stir patriotic feelings and induce civilians to buy bonds to fund America's war effort. Nearly two-thirds of the cost of World War I was paid for by citizens who bought savings bonds and stamps.

The Mood of War

President Wilson had resisted going to war in part because he feared the changes war would bring to America. He once said "lead these people into war and they'll forget there ever was such a thing as tolerance. To fight you must be brutal and ruthless, and the spirit of ruthless brutality will enter into the very fibre of our national life, infecting Congress, the policeman, the man in the street."[57]

His fears were realized. The war resulted in increased discrimination against immigrants, especially those from enemy lands, and brutal suppression of anyone who disagreed with the war or how it was being conducted.

Roosevelt and other backers of preparedness had attacked what the former president called "hyphenated Americans," mostly German American and Austrian American residents or citizens who supported U.S. neutrality.

In leading the preparedness fight Roosevelt said what was needed was "100 percent Americanism" from every citizen. "The professors of every form of hyphenated Americanism are as truly the foes of this country as if they dwelled outside its borders and made active war against it," he charged. "They play the part of traitors, pure and simple. Once it was true that this country could not endure half free and half slave. Today it is true that it cannot endure half American and half foreign. The hyphen is incompatible with patriotism."[58]

Naturalized Americans now began to suffer because many people became suspicious of those who did not speak English and felt sure that anyone who was of German or Austrian descent was a traitor. At times the discrimination was humorous—sauerkraut was called "liberty cabbage," German measles became "liberty measles," and dachshunds were renamed "liberty pups."

But many states passed laws outlawing speaking a foreign language in public, prohibited concerts of German music, burned books written in German, and banned German language instruction in schools. Some foreign workers were fired simply because their employers assumed they were not loyal to America and many innocent citizens were brutally treated.

In Corpus Christi, Texas, a German pastor was whipped for preaching in German and in Wisconsin a German immigrant who had fought for the Union in the Civil War was declared an "enemy alien" when he could not produce his naturalization papers. The worst incident occurred in Collinsville, Illinois, when a mob killed Robert Praeger by hanging him from a tree after denouncing him as a spy. He had become an object of suspicion because he had not enlisted, but papers discovered in his home after his death showed he had tried to join the army but had been rejected because he was blind in one eye.

When the leaders of the Illinois mob were acquitted of charges one of the jurors commented, "Well, I guess nobody can say we aren't loyal now."[59]

Federal Suppression of First Amendment Rights

When war was declared, *Mc-Clure's* magazine stated "the coming 'ism is not Socialism; the coming 'ism is Patriotism."[60] Wilson would allow no dissent on the war and Congress basically rescinded the First Amendment right to free speech by passing the Espionage Act (1917) and the Sedition Act (1918).

The Espionage Act penalized anyone who aided the enemy or obstructed recruiting. It also authorized the postmaster general to ban from the mails any material deemed treasonous or seditious. The Sedition Act made it a crime to say anything to discourage the purchase of war bonds or to speak, print, write, or publish any disloyal or negative material about the government or the war.

Socialists, Industrial Workers of the World, and other radical groups continued to oppose the war even after the United States entered the conflict, claiming it was being fought by capitalists for economic gain at the expense of average citizens who had nothing to gain from the war and who would be sacrificed in battle.

German citizens suspected of being disloyal are herded into a police van in New York City in 1917. In its attempt to crush all opposition to the war, the government violated the civil rights of thousands of people, including hundreds of immigrants who were deported to their former homelands.

Both acts were actively enforced. Socialist Eugene V. Debs was sentenced to ten years in prison for a vaguely antiwar speech in which he said, "You need to know that you are fit for something other than slavery and cannon fodder."[61] The editors of the black newspaper *Messenger* in New York were sentenced to two and one-half years for running a story titled "Pro-Germanism Among Negroes." Socialist congressman Victor Berger of Milwaukee was sentenced to twenty years for helping edit the antiwar Socialist *Milwaukee Leader,* which criticized U.S. participation in the war.

Altogether the acts resulted in some six thousand arrests and fifteen hundred convictions, some for as trivial an offense as contributing a quarter at an antiwar rally.

When a calmer mood returned after the war many of the sentences were overturned or shortened. In 1919 Congress refused to seat Berger, who had been reelected the previous November just six days before the war ended. In 1922, after his conviction was overturned, Berger was elected again and this time allowed to take his seat. In 1920 Debs's sentence was reduced to three years. While he was still in prison in 1920 he received more than nine hundred thousand votes in that year's presidential election.

Boom Times for Workers

Even before the United States entered the war, the U.S. economy had been strengthened by Allied spending. The resulting high demand for workers gave them more leverage in dealing with employers, resulting in higher pay and better working conditions. Their lives had also improved because of Progressive legislation that was creating shorter working hours and addressing workplace issues.

When the nation joined the conflict the National War Labor Board supported higher pay and reduced hours for workers in firms with war contracts. The AFL and many other unions pledged not to strike during the war, which won them more ac-

ceptance by industry. However, although AFL membership grew from 2.7 million in 1916 to more than 4 million in 1917, the gains were temporary and unions lost ground after the war.

The more radical IWW was actively prosecuted by the federal government because of its opposition to the war. On September 5, 1917, the Department of Justice raided all the offices of the IWW in western states and arrested 160 union members on charges of violating the Espionage Act because the union opposed the war. More than 100 Wobblies, including union chief Bill Haywood, were convicted and sentenced to up to twenty years in prison.

When the home of a wealthy Oklahoma oilman was damaged by a bomb soon after the arrests, the IWW was believed to be involved. The *Tulsa World* newspaper, indicating the anti-IWW mood, wrote: "The first step in the whipping of Germany is to strangle the I.W.W.'s. Kill 'em just as you would any other kind of snake. And kill 'em dead." [62]

Black Migration

World War I created many changes in American culture, but perhaps the most significant and long lasting of which was the historic mass migration of blacks to northern cities. This population shift was made possible by the booming war economy centered in the Midwest and Northeast. Companies needed workers so badly

Jeannette Rankin: Pacifist Congresswoman

Jeannette Rankin is proof that lightning can strike twice—at least in politics.

On April 2, 1917, Rankin became the first woman sworn in as a member of Congress. Just four days later the Montana Republican had to cast one of the most difficult votes in history. Elected by supporters of her pacifist views, Rankin was one of fifty House members who voted against declaring war. She passed on the first roll call but on the second stood up and, her voice breaking with emotion, announced: "I want to stand by my country, but I cannot vote for war."

Her "no" vote led to her defeat in the next election but, in one of the supreme ironies in U.S. history, her pacifist views won her another trip to Washington in 1940. The scenario was the same as in 1916—the United States was wavering on whether to enter World War II on the side of the Allies. But once again the situation changed dramatically after she was elected.

A day after the Japanese attacked Pearl Harbor on December 7, 1941, President Franklin D. Roosevelt made a dramatic speech asking Congress to declare war on Japan. Every member of Congress voted "yes"—every member, that is, except Rankin who once again held true to her pacifist principles and voted "no." Once again Rankin was harshly criticized for her vote and defeated in the next election.

Jeannette Rankin, a confirmed pacifist from Montana, is the only member of Congress to vote against fighting in both World War I and World War II. She was a member of the House of Representatives both times Congress voted to declare war.

Jeannette Rankin: the first woman elected to Congress and the only member of Congress to vote against fighting in both World War I and World War II.

that they set aside prejudice and began hiring blacks.

In 1914 nine out of ten blacks lived in the South but in the next five years 500,000 men and women headed north in search of better jobs and more freedom. They were urged to move by labor recruiters, usually blacks, who roamed the South in search of workers and by black newspapers like the

Chicago Defender, which promised them a better life in the North.

Blacks who came down with "northern fever" fled Alabama, Georgia, Mississippi, and other southern states by the tens of thousands. A Department of Labor report during the war stated, "A Negro minister may have all his deacons with him for the mid-week meeting but by Sunday every church officer was likely to be in the North."[63] Most headed for big cities; between 1910 and 1920 the black population in Chicago grew from 44,000 to 109,000, in New York City from 92,000 to 153,000, and in Detroit from 5,700 to 41,000. But for the first time blacks also moved in great numbers to western states, especially California.

Blacks left the South because they were restricted in the jobs they could hold (55 percent of all black males in the South in 1910 were farmers, mostly tenant farmers working for white owners, and 21 percent were domestic servants), denied their rights by Jim Crow segregation laws, and brutally treated. The *Tifton Gazette* in Georgia said blacks were leaving because whites had

> allowed Negroes to be lynched, five at a time, on nothing stronger than suspicion. . . . They have allowed them to be whitecapped and whipped and their homes burned. Loss of much of the State's best labor is one of the prices Georgia is paying for unchecked mob activity against Negroes often charged only with ordinary crimes.[64]

In the North blacks generally fared better economically, were able to vote and send their children to better schools, and could live with more freedom. But northern whites did not accept them as equals and blacks still lived in segregated areas like Harlem in New York.

Women Workers

The same need for workers that sparked the movement of blacks to northern cities gave women new opportunities. In the first years of the new century more and more women had joined the workforce and by 1910 about 7.5 million women held jobs. During the war another million women joined their ranks, many of them filling a

Charles Knight (center) and his riveting crew. The demand for workers was so great during World War I that American industries, sometimes on orders from the U.S. government, abandoned their refusal to hire black workers. Once the war was over, however, most blacks lost the good jobs they had as returning white soldiers reentered the labor market.

Women riveters at the navy yard in Puget Sound, Washington. The need for more workers during World War I gave women a chance at occupations they had never been allowed to try in the past. Although women workers did a good job at whatever they tried, most lost their positions when the war ended.

wide variety of positions formerly denied them. Women were hired in shipyards, ammunition factories, and other wartime industries. They chopped down trees, directed traffic, and became bank tellers and bank managers.

The federal government became a big booster of wartime women workers as well as a big employer. "Not Just Hats Off to the Flag but Sleeves up for It!" proclaimed one patriotic poster that told women it was their patriotic duty to work.

When the United States went to war, President Wilson was not the only one worried about how war would affect the mood of the American people. "I knew, as I knew as I lived," wrote Oswald Garrison Villard, "that this ended the Republic as we had known it; that henceforth we Americans were to be part and parcel of world politics, rivalries, jealousies, and militarism; that hated prejudice and passion were now enthroned in the United States."[65]

He was correct. The war did create a great deal of bitterness, suspicion, and hatred in Americans that did not go away once the war was over.

Chapter Six

French troops look out on opposing German soldiers from their fortifications on the Marne River, scene of several bloody battles during World War I. The Allies had been fighting for three years before the United States entered the war.

The United States Helps Win the War

By the time the United States began fighting in World War I, the Allies were in a desperate situation. Their soldiers were demoralized by the long war, their governments were nearly bankrupted by the costs of war supplies, and Russia, whose huge army had battled the Central Powers so successfully on the eastern front, was in the throes of the Bolshevik revolution.

But the most serious problem was that in the spring of 1917 German submarines were sinking ships bound from America at an intolerable rate. Measured in tons—the unit used to calculate the size of ships—the U-boats sank 563,000 tons in February, 603,000 tons in March, and nearly 900,000 tons in April. The Allies could not build ships as fast as U-boats were sinking them, and sunken shipments of armaments and supplies were critical losses.

But the solution to the U-boat threat was relatively easy once the United States entered the war. Merchant ships had been crossing the Atlantic singly in hopes of evading submarines even though once spotted they were nearly defenseless.

Rear Admiral William S. Sims suggested that destroyers and cruisers protect convoys of merchant ships on their journey. Lookouts on military ships would be able to spot the submarines by their periscopes and strike first. Submarines of the era were vulnerable because they were not very strongly built and had to operate very near the surface.

The convoy strategy proved successful and monthly losses were never again higher than three hundred thousand tons. The United States also extended additional credit for Allied purchases until American soldiers could join the fighting, which would take many months.

A War Like No Other

World War I was a war like none ever fought before. Past wars had been based on movements of opposing armies from one area to another punctuated by fierce, brief battles. But World War I was characterized by a static form of combat that came to be known as trench warfare.

In September 1914 French and British soldiers finally stopped the initial German advance in the Battle of the Marne. Weary of fighting, both sides began to fortify their lines by digging trenches. Little did they know that the trenches would become their homes for five long years of bloody warfare. The western front, a line of trenches four hundred miles long from Switzerland north to the English Channel, became a nearly immovable battle line as neither side could manage a major breakthrough.

Millions of soldiers lived and fought in the trenches, which were separated by a devastated "no-man's-land" sometimes only a few hundred feet wide. Advancing troops on either side had to run across

Allied troops huddle in the trenches that became their homes during World War I. The trenches, uncomfortable even in good weather, were infested with bugs, rats, and disease.

no-man's-land directly into fire from troops in the opposing trenches. If one army did manage to win a few hundred yards of new territory, the opposing soldiers simply fell back and dug new trenches. In this way the same piece of shell-shocked land was fought over time and time again.

Casualty rates were unbelievably high in trench warfare. In the First Battle of Ypres in October 1914 nearly 250,000 soldiers were killed and in the spring of 1915 at Champagne 50,000 Allied soldiers gave their lives to advance five hundred yards. A battle in the same area in September resulted in the deaths of 242,000 Allied soldiers and 141,000 Germans.

Even when neither side was mounting a direct attack, the trenches were hellish places where soldiers spent months at a time before they could go behind the lines for a break. When it rained water poured into the trenches and the earth barricades and makeshift huts soldiers lived in turned to mud, often collapsing around them. In winter they froze. There was no place to relax and no place unexposed to deadly fire from snipers and occasional artillery attacks.

The food was inadequate and usually cold. The trenches, overrun with rats and insects, became a breeding ground for diseases like cholera: More than half the U.S. fatalities were caused by disease, not combat wounds.

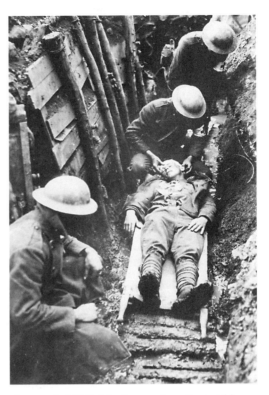

A wounded U.S. Marine receives first aid before being sent to a hospital behind the lines in the Toulon Sector in France in March 1918. More American soldiers died from disease during the war than from combat wounds.

Although the most significant battles were on the western front, World War I was the first war that was truly global. On the eastern front (not characterized by trench warfare) the Russians, Serbians, and other Allied troops attacked the vast Austro-Hungarian Empire as well as Turkish possessions to the east. The clear dominance of the British navy meant the Central Powers risked few naval battles.

The war also shifted to Africa, Asia, and the South Pacific as colonial combatants from six continents took sides in the conflict. In what was known as German East Africa, modern-day Malawi, fighting raged through most of the war. Germany, France, England, and other nations forced Africans in the colonies they controlled to fight even though the land they were fighting over had already been taken away from them. The French also brought Africans to Europe to fight as well as laborers from Indochina. The British recruited soldiers from Canada, Australia, and India.

The Doughboys

Although the draft effectively raised an army it was no easy task turning millions of raw recruits into "doughboys," the WWI nickname for soldiers. Recruits in the American Expeditionary Force were drilled for six months in one of sixteen new military camps, half in southern and half in northern states. The army at first was unprepared for the flood of recruits and lacked weapons and even uniforms. Many recruits wore their own clothing, and even reissued ancient blue Civil War uniforms, for weeks.

After touring military camps as an interested citizen, former president Theodore Roosevelt lashed out at conditions there. "The enormous majority of our men in the encampments," he complained, "were drilling with broomsticks or else with crudely whittled guns. In the camps I saw barrels mounted on stocks on which zeal-

American soldiers at Camp Bowie in Forth Worth, Texas, practice using bayonets. Although the United States declared war on Germany in 1917, it took a year before large numbers of American troops could be trained and sent to France to provide significant help in fighting the war.

Women in War

Although women were not allowed in combat, thousands of American women served in the military by handling noncombat duties such as clerical work. In early 1917 Secretary of the Navy Josephus Daniels said that if the nation enrolled women "in the naval service as yeomen . . . we will have the best clerical assistance the country can provide." Some eleven thousand "yeomanettes" answered the call.

One was Estelle Kemper of Virginia, quoted in *American Women of World War I,* who enlisted and reported to work on the same day. "By nightfall, I felt like an old hand. After dinner I phoned my family in Richmond [Virginia]. My father answered the phone and I told him proudly that I had joined the Navy. Never immune to my bombshells, he gulped and said quickly, 'I'll call your mother.' When I repeated my announcement to her, she was stunned into silence. The poor dear probably saw me in bell-bottomed trousers, swabbing decks, keeping close to the rail, for I was not born to the sea!"

The Army Signal Corps recruited hundreds of telephone operators who could speak French. Shipped to France to handle military phones, they became known as the "Hello Girls." Members of the Women's Army

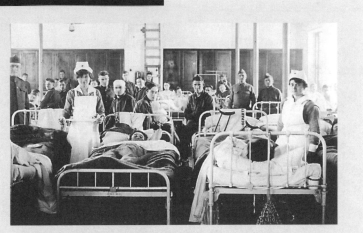

Nurses tend wounded soldiers in an American hospital in Blois, France. Although the United States did not allow women to fight, thousands of American women served overseas as nurses, truck and ambulance drivers, and clerical workers to free men for combat.

Motor Corps delivered supplies, drove doctors to hospitals, transported patients, and handled other transportation duties.

Several thousand members of the Army Nurse Corps tended wounded soldiers. In a letter home from France, quoted in *Multicultural Portrait of World War I,* Julia C. Stimson, a head nurse, exulted over her experience: "To be in the first group of women ever called out for duty with the United States Army, and in the first part of the Army ever sent off on an expeditionary affair of this kind, is all too much good fortune for any one person."

ous captains were endeavoring to teach their men how to ride a horse."[66] Training slowly improved during 1917 as adequate supplies began to arrive.

The draft and enlistments brought together young men with widely different backgrounds, from college graduates to illiterate black and white youths from rural areas, as well as tens of thousands of immigrants, some barely able to speak English, who had been promised citizenship for volunteering.

Black Soldiers

The more than 370,000 blacks who served in the military found the same segregated world they had known as civilians. Their officers were usually white and they bore racist treatment from many white soldiers. Racial tension led to clashes between black and white soldiers and even full-scale riots at military bases and nearby towns.

The worst incident occurred August 21, 1917, in Houston, Texas where the 24th Infantry, an African American unit with a proud military history, was guarding a construction site. When off-duty black soldiers went into town, citizens yelled racial slurs and beat them. After complaints to their superiors failed to correct the problem, Sergeant Vida Henry led a group of about one hundred armed black soldiers into Houston, where they fought with police and civilians. In the ensuing riot twenty-six people died, most of them white. The army severely punished the black soldiers, court-martialing sixty-three of them on charges including disobeying orders, aggravated assault, mutiny, and murder. Nineteen soldiers were hanged and the remaining forty-four sentenced to life imprisonment.

The Tide Turns

On July 4, 1917, after parading through the streets of Paris, the first small contingent of the AEF went to the tomb of the marquis de Lafayette, the French nobleman who had

Members of the all-black 15th Regimental Infantry Division who fought in France. Although blacks were segregated in the armed forces and most were denied the opportunity to engage in combat, tens of thousands of black soldiers performed well during the fighting in World War I.

helped America win its independence in the Revolutionary War. "Lafayette, we are here,"[67] said Colonel Charles E. Stanton. The message was clear—the United States had arrived to pay its debt to its French ally.

Although the French hailed the token band of soldiers as saviors, it was not until the spring of 1918 that enough Americans arrived to play a major role in combat. For six months prior to that the recruits—they were called "rookies," a term used today in sports for first-year professional players—learned to drill, shoot, dig trenches, and fight with bayonets. Military life was a shock, as these popular Irving Berlin lyrics teased:

> Oh! How I hate to get up in the
>   morning,
> Oh! How I'd love to remain in bed;
> For the hardest blow of all
> Is to hear the bugler call—
> "You've got to get up,
> You've got to get up,
> You've got to get up this morning!"[68]

Finally they boarded troop ships for France, where they trained for two more months in war tactics and then spent a month in a quiet sector to learn about life in the trenches. After that they were moved to areas where they would have to fight.

By March 1918 there were still only a

U.S. soldiers appear joyous as they leave for France on a troop ship. The draft put millions of U.S. civilians into uniform and shipped them overseas within a matter of months.

few hundred thousand American soldiers in France. But by July the first million soldiers had come ashore and by October the second million had landed. In all more than 2.2 million American soldiers went overseas. Allied troops were amazed and delighted as truckload after truckload of Americans arrived, spiritedly singing songs as they rode to the front and the trenches.

The arrival of U.S. forces was timely. By the end of 1917 Russia had quit fighting. The Bolsheviks had overthrown Czar Nicholas II and decided to seek peace with Germany. The absence of the huge Russian army on the eastern front allowed Germany to shift nearly a million soldiers to the western front.

The first American troops in France were assigned as replacements in the Allied armies. The first major campaign U.S. soldiers fought in was Cambrai, from November 20 to December 4, 1917.

But in 1918 General Pershing demanded his troops fight as a single force under his own command. The Allies resisted this demand but Pershing prevailed.

Bolstered by huge numbers of Ameri-

Dogfights and Airplanes

The most romantic figures of World War I were pilots, daring young men who flew flimsy aircraft into battle only a little more than a decade after the first historic flight by the Wright brothers in 1903.

At first airplanes were used only to scout and photograph enemy lines and positions. But airplanes quickly won an expanded role in dropping bombs on the enemy and using machine guns to fire on ground troops. The Germans also used zeppelins, large balloonlike aircraft filled with lighter-than-air gas, to bomb cities.

In the early years of the war pilots armed with pistols and rifles engaged in aerial duels that came to be called dogfights. This form of combat was taken to new heights when Roland Garros, a French pilot, mounted a machine gun on his plane. He quickly shot down five enemy planes to earn the nickname "ace of all flyers." After that any pilot who shot down five enemy planes was called an ace. One of the young fliers who was killed in combat was Quentin Roosevelt, youngest son of former president Theodore Roosevelt.

Manfred von Richthofen, dubbed the Red Baron, shot down eighty enemy aircraft. The top ace for the United States was Eddie Rickenbacker, who had twenty-six aerial victories. Frank Luke Jr. won the nickname Balloon Buster for shooting down fifteen German observation balloons and his total of twenty-one kills made him the second-ranking U.S. ace.

The American fliers were commanded by General William "Billy" Mitchell, who in the 1920s would prove that airplanes dropping bombs could sink ships. The Army Air Service

Lieutenant Earl Carroll, one of the U.S. pilots who helped inaugurate a new, deadly form of combat in World War I, the use of airplanes. The daring young men who engaged in aerial combat became the most romantic figures of the war.

was poorly prepared when World War I started but by the end of the war Mitchell commanded a force of nearly fifteen hundred airplanes. Some of the best U.S. pilots had been fighting in France since 1916 with the Lafayette Escadrille, a group of Americans attached to the French Flying Corps. When America entered the war they switched to the Army Air Service so they could fight for their country.

can soldiers, the Allies now had a manpower advantage and Pershing's doughboys played a major role in throwing back German challenges at Château-Thierry, Belleau Wood, and Reims. Allied forces also broke out of the trenches to attack the Germans strongly at St. Mihiel and in the Meuse-Argonne region.

The most significant American engagement came in September 1918 when 1.2 million Americans swarmed out of the trenches west of Verdun and, side by side with British and French troops, pushed the Germans back into the Argonne Forest. The fighting raged for more than a month but the Allies kept gaining ground and forcing the Germans closer to surrender.

Black Regiments

Almost 90 percent of black soldiers, including the 200,000 sent to Europe, had to serve in labor battalions or other noncombat positions because white officers claimed they were incapable of fighting. General W. H. Hay cited what he believed to be "the inherent weaknesses in Negro character, especially generally a lack of intelligence and initiative." Robert L. Bullard, commander of the Second Army, wrote after the war that "the average Negro is a rank coward in the dark" and said "they are hopelessly inferior."[69]

They held this view despite the fact that 5,000 blacks had fought in the Revolutionary War, 3,000 in the War of 1812, and almost 200,000 in the Civil War. And the black soldiers who did make it to combat proved themselves individually and as a unit.

The mostly black 369th Regiment earned the nickname "Hell Fighters" for its ferocity. The regiment was under fire for 191 days without relief, suffering more than 1,500 casualties. The regiment was awarded the Croix de Guerre, France's highest military honor, for its gallantry.

A June 1918 United Press news story praised black soldiers in the 93rd Division. "In the midst of this inferno," the report said, "the Negroes coolly stuck to their posts, operating machine guns and automatic rifles and keeping up such a steady barrage that the Germany infantry failed to penetrate the American lines."[70]

Wilson as Peacemaker

From the start of the war President Wilson had believed it was the duty of the United States to bring peace to the world. He had made several unsuccessful attempts to convince the two sides to stop fighting; on January 18, 1918, with American troops already in France, he made another plea. In a speech to Congress Wilson outlined a framework for a lasting peace that became known as the Fourteen Points.

Wilson insisted any peace agreement would have to be openly arrived at, meaning an end to the kind of secret agreements between nations that helped start the war. The Fourteen Points demanded arms reductions by all countries, establishment of new nations from the remains of the Austro-Hungarian and Ottoman Empires, creation of an independent Poland, and an end to imperialism.

Wilson's final point was his most daring: He proposed the creation of a new international organization to prevent future wars, an idea resulting in the League of Nations, the predecessor to the United Nations.

On February 11 the president clarified his Fourteen Points with an additional Four Points, the most volatile of which was self-determination. It stated "national aspirations must be respected; peoples may now be dominated and governed only by their own consent. 'Self-determination' is not a mere phrase; it is an imperative principle of action."[71] This meant that more powerful nations should not be allowed to rule weaker countries or groups of people against their wishes.

George Creel, who headed the Committee on Public Information, had advised Wilson to present his proposals as simple points so people around the world could easily understand them. He now disseminated the Fourteen Points to every corner of the globe, including copies in German that were showered on enemy soldiers via artillery shells. The idea was to convince German soldiers to quit fighting by showing them the United States wanted a just end to the war. The propaganda campaign worked so well that some German soldiers, already demoralized by long years of war, began to surrender.

However, neither Allied nor Central Power leaders responded positively to Wilson's message and the war dragged on.

Armistice

As the Allies were smashing through the German lines on October 3, Wilson sent another diplomatic note to Germany requesting an armistice based on his Fourteen Points. Faced with impending defeat, the German generals agreed to negotiate but it took more than a month for the two sides to reach an agreement.

On November 9 Kaiser Wilhelm II relinquished the German throne and fled to Holland. Two days later, on November 11 at 11 A.M., the fighting ended and the guns fell silent for the first time since August 1914.

World War I caused the deaths of more people than any previous war in history. The Allies suffered 5.1 million deaths and the Central Powers nearly 3.4 million. The United States, which fought for less than two years, suffered some 116,000 deaths and nearly 200,000 were wounded. Great Britain and its colonies incurred 947,000 deaths, France 1.38 million, and Russia 1.7 million. Germany lost 1.8 million soldiers, Austria-Hungary 1.2 million, and Turkey 325,000. About 20 million soldiers were wounded in the fighting.

Millions of civilians were also killed. Estimates vary but it is believed as many as 10 million civilians died in the war, many from starvation.

The Treaty of Versailles

At war's end Wilson made a historic decision—he would attend the peace talks in France, the first time a president had ever visited Europe to meet with other heads of state. Wilson left New York on December 4, 1919, on the *George Washington* and nine days later arrived in France to a hero's welcome by large crowds cheering "Vive le President Wilson!"

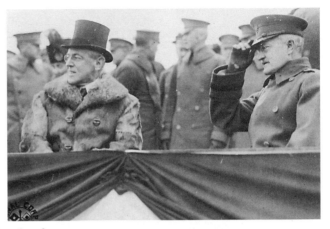

President Woodrow Wilson (left in top hat) and General John J. Pershing. Wilson went to Europe when the fighting was over to help leaders of other nations work out formal peace treaties.

His reception by Allied leaders was less enthusiastic. French premier Georges Clemenceau, Prime Minister David Lloyd George of Great Britain, and Prime Minister Vittorio Orlando of Italy all resented Wilson and America's new status as a world power and felt Wilson had been arrogant in trying to dictate terms to end a war in which their countries had sacrificed so much more than America. Clemenceau said dryly of the president: "Mr. Wilson bores me with his Fourteen Points; why, God almighty has only ten!"[72]

These three leaders and Wilson, collectively known as the Big Four, battled sharply over the treaty. Wilson had a grand vision of a just peace that would end all future threat of war but the Euro-

pean leaders hated Germany and wanted vengeance. During breaks in the talks Lloyd George and Clemenceau visited nearby battlefields to refresh their minds of the horror the Germans had caused.

The most contentious issue was the huge war damages European leaders wanted Germany to pay. Clemenceau, who had lived through two German invasions, said: "The greater the bloody catastrophe which devastated and ruined one of the richest regions of France, the more ample and splendid should be the reparation."[73]

Wilson, who hated to compromise, gave in over and over again to win support for the League of Nations. Wilson agreed to impose billions of dollars in German reparations, to disarm Germany alone and not all nations, and to give Germany's holdings to the other powers.

Wilson's plea for self-determination had raised the hopes of millions of people around the world for freedom from colonial rule but Wilson lost this battle too. For the most part the Big Four ignored this idea in dividing up land held by Germany and the Austro-Hungarian and Ottoman Empires.

Some ethnic groups, such as the Polish, were granted independence, but the victorious European nations were allowed to maintain their colonies around the world and granted control of land formerly ruled by the Central Powers. This disappointed representatives of various nations and ethnic groups who had come to Paris to plead their cases for independence.

Among them was Ho Chi Minh of Vietnam, who sought an end to French rule in Indochina. Like many others, Ho was unsuccessful; nationalist rebellion would characterize Vietnam for another fifty years.

The Treaty of Versailles, which dealt only with Germany, was signed June 28, 1919, in the Hall of Mirrors at Versailles, the historic French palace. The Allies agreed to terms with Austria-Hungary, Bulgaria, and the Ottoman Empire in separate treaties.

The Versailles agreement forced Germany to pay the Allies $56 billion and stripped it of about 10 percent of its land in Europe as well as colonies in China, the South Pacific, and Africa. The treaty created nine new nations, four of them carved from the Austro-Hungarian Empire— Austria, Czechoslovakia, Hungary, and Yugoslavia. Other new countries were Poland, Latvia, Lithuania, Estonia, and Finland.

The Treaty of Sevres dealt with the Ottoman Empire. The Allies had already reached secret agreements on which nation would gain control of the empire's territories and Wilson had little choice but to go along with them. Finalized in 1920, the treaty gave England and France control of the former empire's Arabic-speaking holdings in the Middle East and Africa, which included Palestine and Egypt. It also made Armenia a free nation.

The League of Nations

Significantly, the Treaty of Versailles established the League of Nations, an international body with an assembly of representatives from every member nation and an executive council of nine countries, including the United States, Great Britain, France, Italy, and Japan. The League also comprised a Secretariat to provide administrative functions, a World Court to rule on disputes between nations, and special commissions to deal with specific problems.

The most important section of the League's covenant was Article 10, which called for each nation "to respect and

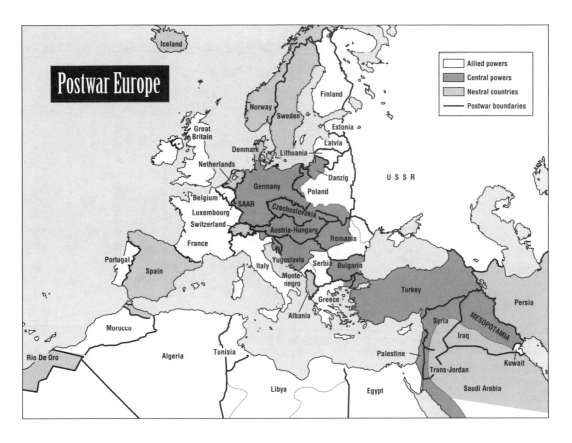

Postwar Europe

	Allied powers
	Central powers
	Neutral countries
—	Postwar boundaries

preserve as against external aggression the territorial integrity and existing political independence of all members of the league."[74]

This was the function of the League of Nations that Wilson felt would prevent future wars. The League was his dream,

the accomplishment he valued more than any other in his illustrious career. But although Woodrow Wilson had helped win World War I, he was about to lose the battle for the League of Nations in his own country.

Chapter Seven

*American civilians gleefully celebrate the end of World War I.
However, the joy that came from defeating Germany gave way to
a postwar period of gloom as prices rose, the peacetime economy
faltered, labor problems erupted, and the aftermath of the war left
many Americans bitter over having taken part in the conflict.*

The Postwar Period

The Allied victory in World War I had a strange effect on the United States. Instead of exultation, Americans felt disillusionment over the Great War. The idealism that had energized the Progressive movement and characterized most of Wilson's domestic and foreign policies was replaced by an emotional letdown, cynicism, and negativity. Supreme Court Justice Louis D. Brandeis once said, "Europe was devastated by war, we by the aftermath."[75]

Americans were horrified by the deaths and injuries to U.S. soldiers, even though they were a fraction of those suffered by other nations. They were angered by a perceived Allied lack of gratitude for America's role in victory and, worse, by what seemed to be Allied foot dragging in repaying war loans. Some people blamed big business, which had profited from the war, for causing it. Most of all, Americans were still filled with the negative emotions the war had produced.

The result was that the final year of the twentieth century's second decade was a bitter time. Labor strife, held in patriotic check by wartime necessity, erupted in a series of strikes because of spiraling inflation. Hundreds of thousands of soldiers returned home needing jobs, resulting in short-term massive unemployment as the economy made the bumpy switch from war to peace. The anti-immigrant sentiment created by the war was escalated by the economic problems and fear of Communists, who had swept to power in Russia in a bloody revolution. The movement of hundreds of thousands of blacks to northern cities created new racial problems and helped fuel the rebirth of the Ku Klux Klan. The nation that had so purposefully gone to war now wanted to retreat into isolationism.

Wilson Loses the Peace

Woodrow Wilson returned home expecting to win easy approval of the Treaty of Versailles. Instead he was confronted by senators who wanted no part of a new world order that included his beloved League of Nations.

Republican senators were also spoiling for a fight with the Democratic president on grounds of party politics. They were angry that Wilson had not taken a high-ranking Republican to the peace talks and that he had used the war as political capital. Before the November 1918 congressional election Wilson had urged voters to elect Democrats because "a Republican majority would be interpreted on the other side of the water as repudiation of my leadership."[76] Republicans who had loyally supported a Democratic president during the war felt betrayed. The public agreed and responded by electing a Republican majority in the Senate.

Republican senators led by Henry Cabot Lodge opposed League membership because they believed it would weaken America. Senator William Borah, an Idaho Republican who was a Progressive on most issues, asked, "Why should we interweave our destiny with the European destiny?" Borah said the League did not discriminate between American and European affairs and claimed "the very object and purpose of the league is to eliminate all differences between Europe and America and to place all in a common liability to be governed and controlled by a common authority."[77]

Lodge, in mockery of Wilson's Fourteen Points, suggested "Fourteen Reservations" to the treaty. He objected that the agreement did not recognize special U.S. rights in Latin America under the Monroe Doctrine; did not say member nations had control of their own internal affairs; did not give member nations the right to withdraw from the League; and did not acknowledge that Congress had to approve any League-mandated action the United States would be party to.

Wilson decided to take his appeal directly to voters: He left Washington on September 3, 1919, on an eight-thousand-mile railroad journey in which he made thirty-five speeches in twenty-two days. In Omaha he said League membership was vital to the world's future: "I tell you, my fellow citizens, I can predict with absolute certainty that within another generation, there will be another world war if the nations of the world do not concert the method by which to prevent it."[78]

But on September 26, en route to Wichita, Kansas, Wilson became ill. The president was rushed back to Washington where he suffered a stroke that left him an invalid. For more than two months his left side was paralyzed, his speech blurred, his vision drastically reduced. Mentally confused as well, Wilson saw no one during this period except his wife, Edith, and Cary Grayson, his personal physician. He signed whatever papers were put before him and did not meet with his cabinet for six months. His illness left the nation without a leader.

Wilson never completely recovered and was physically weak and politically ineffective for the rest of his presidency. On November 19, 1919, Senate Republicans took advantage of his absence to reject the Treaty of Versailles. The Senate voted it down again on March 19, 1920, returning the pact to Wilson with a formal notice of its inability to ratify the treaty. It is believed that Wilson could have won approval by making minor concessions but was too stubborn to compromise. "Better a thousand times to go down fighting," he told his wife, "than to dip your colors to dishonorable compromise."[79]

The United States finally signed a separate peace treaty with Germany in 1921 that contained the general provisions of the Treaty of Versailles, but the United States never joined the League of Nations.

President Woodrow Wilson while on a national tour to try to win public support for the League of Nations. His great dream of a League of Nations was rejected by his Republican opponents in Congress.

Who Was President?

For several months in the fall of 1919 there was doubt as to who was really guiding the United States. Was President Woodrow Wilson, an invalid following his stroke, able to make decisions on issues presented to him? Or was his wife, Edith, the one who was actually performing the duties of president of the United States?

In *Woodrow Wilson*, historian John Garraty claims that Wilson was so ill that his wife was in effect the head of the nation. It was Mrs. Wilson who on October 2 had gone to his room and discovered he had suffered a stroke. Wilson was near death for two weeks but the public was never informed of his condition.

"During this period," Garraty writes, "Mrs. Wilson was for practical purposes the president of the United States. For another six weeks she, along with Dr. [Cary] Grayson, exerted more influence over the office than Wilson himself, for their decisions determined what business was brought to his attention. Indeed, for the remainder of his term Mrs. Wilson acted as a buffer between her husband and the duties of his office in a way scarcely contemplated by the Constitution."

President Woodrow Wilson and his wife, Edith, look over some papers on the president's desk. When a stroke incapacitated Wilson for several months in 1919, Edith Wilson is believed to have performed some of the duties of the president.

Mrs. Wilson only allowed a few people to see her husband because she worried it would be too taxing physically. "I am not interested in the president of the United States. I am interested in my husband and his health," she would say.

Garraty writes, "The government had no real head; Cabinet members ran their own departments, aided only by an occasional cryptic note scrawled across memoranda they had submitted to the White House." Even when Wilson became stronger, it was difficult for him to function as president.

The Twenty-fifth Amendment to the Constitution, ratified in 1967, outlines procedures in which Congress can elevate the vice president to acting president if the president is "unable to discharge the powers and duties of his office." This constitutional change is intended to avoid a repeat of the situation involving Wilson.

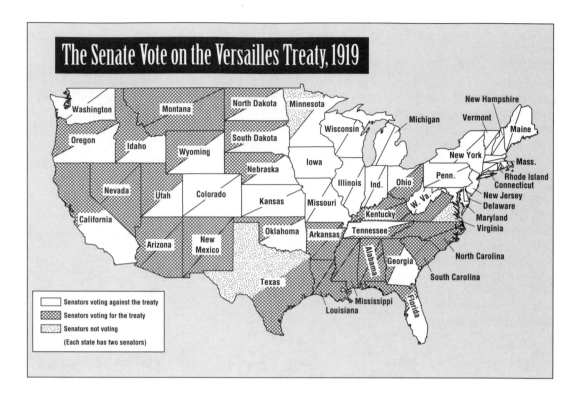

The Senate Vote on the Versailles Treaty, 1919

Senators voting against the treaty

Senators voting for the treaty

Senators not voting

(Each state has two senators)

Labor Problems

In the year after the war ended there were more than three thousand strikes involving 4 million workers. Postwar inflation was high—prices nearly doubled between 1914 and 1919 and were still rising—and workers demanded higher wages. But the public, which had once backed workers in their fight against management, now turned against them. Americans had renewed faith in big business, which had emerged from the war with a brighter reputation because the armaments, food, and other supplies it produced had helped win the war. The business world took advantage of this new political climate to attack labor.

One of the key labor disputes of 1919 was a strike on September 22 by 365,000 steelworkers demanding higher wages and the right to form a union. Sixty percent of the strikers still worked twelve-hour days and the average yearly wage was $1,466 for a sixty-nine-hour week.

Steel companies retaliated by charging that because so many of the workers were immigrants their strike was un-American and by claiming the unions were dominated by radicals. Steel company owners ran newspaper ads that said "Stand by America, Show Up the Red Agitator." Their argument carried a lot of weight because the public had come to fear radicals;

"Reds" and Bolsheviks, many thought, wanted to take over America as they had Russia. This alarm became known as the Red Scare.

During the strike the Senate Committee on Labor accepted such claims without investigating them. It also issued a report that said a "considerable element of IWW's, anarchists, revolutionists, and Russian Soviets" were using the strike "as a means of elevating themselves to power."[80] In fact, there were radicals in the union movement, but most union members were just trying to win better wages and working conditions.

The strike was bitter, with violence on both sides causing the deaths of more than twenty workers. It ended January 8, 1920, when steelworkers went back to work. They had won a few concessions but not union recognition, their main goal.

Boston policemen initiated another key strike on September 9 because they had not had a raise since the war started. When 1,117 of 1,544 patrolmen walked off the job, looting and crime broke out and Massachusetts governor Calvin Coolidge called out the National Guard to restore order. Policemen returned to work but were promptly fired. Boston officials gave the new police officers it hired the wage

hikes and improvements the strikers had requested, making the point that strikers would be punished.

When AFL president Samuel Gompers complained to Coolidge the governor responded sharply: "There is no right to strike against the public safety by anyone, anywhere, any time."[81] His hard line made Coolidge a national figure and he was elected president in 1924.

Massachusetts governor Calvin Coolidge inspects state guardsmen who replaced striking Boston police in 1919. His hard-line stand against striking officers made Coolidge a national hero and later helped him win election as president.

In 1919 President Wilson declared a strike by coal miners in West Virginia violated wartime restrictions on strikes that were still in effect. This allowed the governor of West Virginia to send in state militia to end the strike and hand the miners a dramatic defeat.

The strikes by police and steelworkers began a period of several years of intensive union-busting activities by management. The AFL, whose membership had grown during the war and peaked in 1920 at 5 million, declined to 3.6 million members in 1923 and 2.9 million a decade later.

In postwar America Communists were public enemy number one. Although there were never more than seventy-five thousand active Communists in the United States, Americans developed an irrational fear of communism. Possible Communist takeovers in Germany and Hungary did pose a threat in postwar Europe, where the war had shattered economies and tens of thousands of people were dying of starvation and disease. Though the United States had grown in power and wealth during the war, Americans became fearful Communists would overrun their nation as well.

The driving force behind the Red Scare was Attorney General A. Mitchell Palmer, who in 1919 began a political witch-hunt in which the government ignored the civil rights of the people it set out to prosecute. Palmer organized a series of raids in cities across the country from November 1919 through January 1920. In the 1920 raid some six thousand Socialists, Communists, and other radicals were arrested, including teenage girls only fourteen and sixteen years old. Charged with being criminal anarchists, most were proven innocent and only about 550 were deported.

The Red Scare continued until May 1, 1920, a day on which Palmer predicted violence would flare across the nation because it was the day that Communists celebrated the Russian Revolution. When nothing happened, the Red Scare began to fade.

Anti-Immigrant Feelings

What did not fade was the anti-immigrant feeling that had begun to surface during the war in the calls for "100 percent Americanism" and the discrimination against citizens from Central Power nations reminiscent of the nativism in the mid-1880s when many Americans were suspicious of and resented all immigrants.

Even though the war had slowed immigration to a trickle after 1914, in 1917 Congress passed a bill requiring immigrants to be literate. This measure had been vetoed twice in the past by presidents who felt it was unfair because it was aimed directly at immigrants from eastern and southern Europe, who somehow seemed "undesirable" to many Americans. Wilson vetoed the bill a third time in 1917 but Congress overrode him. The bill reduced

Newly arrived immigrants are tested at Ellis Island, the facility in New York City in which millions of immigrants were processed when they first arrived in the United States. The United States after World War I tightened immigration regulations to limit the number of foreigners who could move to America.

immigration from those areas because many people living there were illiterate.

Anti-immigration efforts were backed by people like novelist Kenneth Roberts, who argued in an article in the *Saturday Evening Post* that unrestricted immigration would flood the nation with "human parasites" and produce "a hybrid race of good-for-nothing mongrels."[82] This was an historic turning point, for the United States had always welcomed immigrants. George Washington once said "the bosom of America is open . . . to the oppressed and persecuted of all nations and religions." And the Statue of Liberty, the first thing new immigrants saw when their ships arrived in New York, bears these lines from the poem by Emma Lazarus: "Give me your tired, your poor, your huddled masses yearning to breathe free."[83]

Racial Violence

Following the war, black Americans felt they had earned the right to better treatment. In 1919 W. E. B. Du Bois wrote in the *Crisis* that America was "yet a shameful land. It *lynches*, it *disfranchises* its citizens, it

encourages *ignorance*, it steals from us, it insults." But he warned America:

We *return*. We *return from fighting*. We *return fighting*. Make way for Democracy! We saved it in France, and by the Great Jehovah, we will save it in the United States of America or know the reason why.[84]

Instead the racial climate became even more hostile. The migration of blacks brought racial problems to new areas of the country because blacks in northern

The body of a black person killed during a race riot in Chicago on June 30, 1919, is placed in a police car. During World War I hundreds of thousands of blacks moved out of their traditional home in the South to northern cities. The postwar period saw a rise in racist activities against blacks living in the North.

cities were now competing with whites for jobs and living space.

Between June 1919 and the end of the year there were twenty-eight race riots across the country, including the worst in the nation's history. In Chicago in June, 38 people were killed, 537 injured, and more than a thousand homes destroyed.

The violence began when Eugene Williams, a young black man, ventured into a beach area on Lake Michigan reserved for whites. When whites stoned Williams until he drowned, blacks and whites began fighting. The violence spread to other parts of Chicago and continued for six days. A grand jury that investigated the incident reported "the colored people suffered more at the hands of white hoodlums than white people suffered at the hands of black hoodlums."[85]

In the first year after the war seventy blacks were lynched or killed, including at least ten who were wearing their World War I uniforms, and some four hundred blacks in all were murdered between 1919 and 1927. The NAACP in 1919 introduced an antilynching bill in Congress but southerners in the Senate staged a filibuster to kill it. The NAACP kept fighting to stop lynchings and they gradually decreased; however, reported lynchings occurred as late as 1960.

A major reason blacks had so little success in improving their living conditions was that they were often denied the right to vote by racist laws. But in 1919

another group, women, finally won their battle for the ballot.

Women's Suffrage

The suffrage movement had intensified during the war and adopted new, more aggressive tactics. Alice Paul began a new group called the Congressional Union

Alice Paul, a social worker and one of the leaders of the suffrage movement, helped women win the right to vote in elections in 1920.

Women's Suffrage

The crusade to win the vote for women began at a convention in 1848 in Seneca Falls, New York, to discuss women's rights. It took seventy-two years and the work of thousands of women to win this important civil rights battle.

Progress was slow for several decades but in 1869 Elizabeth Cady Stanton, an organizer of the historic Seneca Falls meeting, and Susan B. Anthony founded the National Woman Suffrage Association, which worked to secure a constitutional amendment to give women the right to vote. First introduced in Congress in 1878, the measure was defeated.

Suffragette workers register women to vote. For more than a half century women marched, pleaded, organized, protested, and did everything else they could to win the right to vote.

Anthony, the most well known leader of the suffrage movement, also helped found the National American Woman Suffrage Association (NAWSA) and was its president from 1892 to 1900. A Quaker raised by her father to believe in the equality of men and women, she died in 1906 with her goal unrealized. But in 1979 she was honored by the government when she became the first woman to have her likeness appear on a U.S. coin, the Susan B. Anthony silver dollar.

The fight was long and complicated. Carrie Chapman Catt, quoted in *The Day the Women Got the Vote*, and who became NAWSA president in 1900, once capsulized it this way:

"To get the word 'male' in effect out of the Constitution cost the women of the country years of pauseless campaign. During that time they were forced to conduct fifty-six campaigns or referenda to male voters; 480 campaigns to get legislatures to submit suffrage amendments to voters; 47 campaigns to get State constitutional conventions to write woman suffrage into state constitutions; 277 campaigns to get State party conventions to include woman suffrage plans; 30 campaigns to get presidential party conventions to adopt woman suffrage planks in party platforms: and 19 campaigns with 19 successive Congresses."

dedicated to passage of a constitutional amendment to give women the right to vote.

Paul and other suffragists began picketing the White House on January 10, 1917, carrying signs bearing the slogan, "How Long Must Women Wait for Liberty?" They continued picketing for almost a year despite arrests that jailed more than a hundred women, some of whom refused to pay fines and went on hunger strikes. Americans were shocked and angered when newspapers reported that jail officials tried to force-feed the women to end their hunger strike.

The dramatic White House protests during the war and the contributions women made in this period won new support for the suffrage movement. On January 9, 1918 Wilson finally spoke out in support of suffrage and urged passage of the Nineteenth Amendment. A day later the House passed the measure but it took another year to win Senate approval. On August 26, 1920, the amendment was ratified and that November women voted for the first time in a presidential election.

Women were victorious at last. Carrie Chapman Catt, president of the National American Woman Suffrage Association, said, "The greatest thing that came out of the war was the emancipation of women, for which no man fought."[86] Chapman went on to found the League of Women Voters, which helped women learn to use their new political power.

Prohibition

On January 29, 1919, another constitutional amendment went into effect, this time taking away a right instead of bestowing one. The Eighteenth Amendment, which Congress had approved December 18, 1917, prohibited the production, sale, distribution, and consumption of alcohol. On October 28, 1919, Congress passed the Volstead Act, which provided enforcement for the social experiment known as Prohibition. It went into effect January 16, 1920, officially making America a "dry" nation.

The fight for Prohibition had gone on as long as the battle for women's suffrage; in 1851 temperance supporters won their fight to end legal drinking in Maine and by 1900 one out of four Americans lived in areas where saloons were banned. In the 1910s the battle against "demon rum" was waged by the Women's Christian Temperance Union, the Methodist Church, and the Anti-Saloon League.

The Prohibition drive gained strength in the twentieth century for two reasons: (1) the Progressive movement had shown social change was possible through legislation and (2) there had been a dramatic increase in drinking. From 1850 to 1890 beer consumption increased from 36 million to 855 million gallons even though the population only rose from 23 million to 63 million. Prohibitionists blamed the increase on immigrants like the Germans, Irish, and Italians whose cultures tradition-

A delegation from Brooklyn, New York, takes part in a "wet" parade in Washington, D.C., on June 15, 1919, to show their support for the right to drink alcoholic beverages. The Eighteenth Amendment to the Constitution in January 1919 made the manufacture, sale, and consumption of alcoholic beverages illegal.

ally enjoyed beer, wine, and whiskey. They also wanted to close down the thousands of saloons that had sprung up in big cities, claiming the drinking establishments were centers of gambling, prostitution, drug sales, and political corruption.

By the time World War I started over two-thirds of the states were dry and almost three-fourths of Americans lived in areas where they could not legally buy beer or liquor. During the war Prohibitionists stepped up their efforts, claiming the grain used to make alcoholic beverages should be conserved for food.

Prohibitionism proved unsuccessful as well as unpopular, as people kept drinking despite the law. In 1933 the nation's greatest experiment in social engineering ended with passage of the Twenty-first Amendment, which repealed the Eighteenth and made drinking legal again.

A Decade Ends

At the end of the new century's second decade, America's spirit seemed drained by the whirlwind events of the last ten years. The energy, enthusiasm, and idealism that had fueled the nation's efforts in the Progressive movement and in winning World War I seemed to have withered. The negative emotions brought to life by the war, however, lived on and in some cases gained even more strength.

It was an entirely human reaction after an event as traumatic as a war that had consumed the country's hearts and minds for several years. But this emotional letdown would prove to be short for Americans. It would give way to the energy and good times most people would experience in the new decade, which would eventually become known in history as the Roaring Twenties.

President Woodrow Wilson tips his hat to the crowd during a presidential motorcade circa 1916–1917. Although Wilson became one of the most powerful presidents in U.S. history when he was granted special powers during World War I, he left office a broken man.

A Mood of Pessimism

In the second decade of the twentieth century, President Woodrow Wilson dominated events in the United States and the world as few presidents have. Historian Mark Sullivan sums up his immense influence:

"For some five years, 1914–1919, the history of the United States, as respects the Great War, was mainly the history of Woodrow Wilson's mind. For the last two years, 1917–1919, the history of the whole world was the history of Wilson's mind."[87] Along with his victories on Progressive issues in his first term, Wilson emerged from the decade with a long list of remarkable accomplishments.

Yet Wilson left office in 1920 in defeat, his dream for the League of Nations shattered by isolationist Republicans, his party ousted from power by voters who in 1920 elected Republican Warren G. Harding president over Democrat James M. Cox. Following Senate rejection of the Versailles treaty, Wilson finished his term politically powerless and in a constant state of gloom. He was no happier afterward, leading a lonely, embittered life until his death February 3, 1924.

America's Postwar Mood

The nation in general exited the second decade as did Wilson—unhappy, angry, and pessimistic. The editors of the *New Republic,* a Progressive magazine, wrote that "the war did no good to anybody. Those of its generation whom it did not kill, it crippled, wasted, or used up." [88]

World War I has been called the most popular in U.S. history while it lasted and the most hated when it was over. Americans were appalled that so many of their soldiers were killed or wounded. They were angry that the Allied nations were not properly grateful for U.S. help in beating Germany, especially since they owed the United States $10 billion in loans. Americans were also in turmoil because of the unemployment, inflation, and labor problems that plagued the nation following the war.

This postwar gloom, however, was relatively brief. The economy quickly came back to life and Americans were swept away by the gaiety and energy of the decade that became known as the Roaring Twenties. There were even some people who could now find something positive about the war.

Writer Lincoln Steffens said if nothing else the war at least had made Americans realize their nation was great. "We went into the war a conceited, but secretly rather humble, second-rate country," Steffens said. "We came out self-assured. Our soldiers, our engineers, our

Suzette Dewey, daughter of Assistant Secretary of Treasury Charles Dewey, poses with her own automobile.

organizers and managers, our industrialists and financiers—we had measured ourselves with our European competitors and discovered our competence. We were first-rate people, the first world power!"[89]

Wilson's Legacy

The person most responsible for making America "the first world power" was Wilson, a chief executive who not only guided the course of history in his own time but left a challenging legacy for future presidents.

Long before his election Wilson had envisioned how a president should act. The chief executive must become the nation's dominant political figure, someone unafraid to use the power of his office. "His is the only national voice in affairs," Wilson wrote. "Let him win the admiration and confidence of the country and no other single force can withstand him. . . . His office is anything he has the sagacity and force to make it."[90]

Except for his failure with the League of Nations, Wilson fulfilled that vision. By wielding the full powers of the office he held, Wilson seized the leadership role Congress had traditionally held and strengthened the presidency for all time. Every future president would owe Wilson a debt of gratitude.

The Progressive issues Wilson fought for also altered the scope of federal government. By advocating legislation on is-

In his two terms as president, Woodrow Wilson left a strong legacy of leadership for future chief executives while guiding the nation through a difficult period in its history.

sues such as an eight-hour work day and limits on child labor, Wilson directly involved the federal government in creating social change. His New Freedom philosophy—and Roosevelt's New Nationalism, for that matter—was a direct ancestor of Franklin D. Roosevelt's New Deal, Harry Truman's Fair Deal, and Lyndon B. Johnson's Great Society.

The details of all of these programs were quite different but their philosophy was the same—that the federal government had a duty to help its citizens and not just govern them.

The Roots of Another War

Wilson said what bothered him most about his defeat on the treaty was that it meant the United States was retreating into isolation: "We had a chance to gain the leadership of the world. We have lost it, and soon we shall be witnessing the tragedy of it all."[91]

The tragedy was something he had predicted in 1918 on his national tour to drum up support for the treaty—another war.

In 1939, just thirty years after World War I ended, World War II began. The harsh financial reparations Germany had to pay, which Wilson had strongly opposed, ruined its economy and ultimately helped Adolf Hitler come to power. Without the backing of the United States, the League of Nations was too weak to stop events in the thirties from spiraling into another war.

And thus World War I was not to be, as Wilson hoped, the war to end all wars.

Notes

Introduction: A Time of Change

1. Quoted in James MacGregor Burns, *Workshop of Democracy: The American Experiment,* vol. 2. New York: Knopf, 1985, p. 141.
2. Quoted in Ernest R. May, *The Life History of the United States,* vol. 9, *1901–1917.* New York: Time-Life Books, 1974, p.33.

Chapter One: The Progressive Movement and Woodrow Wilson

3. Quoted in Burns, *Workshop of Democracy,* p. 113.
4. Quoted in May, *The Life History of the United States,* p. 54.
5. Quoted in Foster Rhea Dulles, *The United States Since 1865.* Ann Arbor: University of Michigan Press, 1971, p. 205.
6. Quoted in Page Smith, *America Enters the World: A People's History of the Progressive Era and World War I.* New York: McGraw-Hill, 1985, p. 302.
7. Quoted in John A. Garraty, *The American Nation,* vol. 2, *A History of the United States Since 1865.* New York: HarperCollins, 1991, p. 663.
8. Quoted in James West Davidson et al., *Nation of Nations: A Narrative History of the American Republic.* New

York: McGraw-Hill, 1994, p. 862.
9. Quoted in Smith, *America Enters the World,* p. 405.
10. Quoted in Thomas A. Bailey, *The American Pageant,* 5th ed., vol. 2. Lexington, MA: D. C. Heath, 1975, p. 732.
11. Quoted in Dulles, *The United States Since 1865,* p. 215.

Chapter Two: The Fight for Rights

12. Quoted in Davidson et al., *Nation of Nations,* p. 832.
13. Quoted in Thomas R. Brooks, *Toil and Trouble: A History of American Labor,* 2nd ed. New York: Delacorte, 1971, p. 77.
14. Quoted in Julie Roy Jeffrey et al., eds., *The American People: Creating a Nation and Society,* 2nd ed. New York: HarperCollins, 1990, p. 727.
15. Quoted in Smith, *America Enters the World,* p. 476.
16. Quoted in Bailey, *The American Pageant,* p. 523.
17. Quoted in Smith, *America Enters the World,* p. 400.
18. Quoted in Jeffrey et al., *The American People,* p. 742.
19. Quoted in Michael V. Uschan, *A Multicultural Portrait of World War I.* New York: Marshall Cavendish, 1996, p. 19.

20. Quoted in Jeffrey et al., *The American People,* p. 599.

21. Quoted in Garraty, *The American Nation,* p. 668.

22. Quoted in Bailey, *The American Pageant,* p. 707.

Chapter Three: Popular Culture: Silent Films, Vaudeville, and the Model T

23. Quoted in Marshall B. Davidson, *Life in America,* vol. 2. Boston: Houghton Mifflin, 1951, p. 82.

24. Quoted in Maitland A. Edey, ed., *This Fabulous Century,* vol. 2, *1910–1920.* New York: Time-Life Books, 1969, p. 56.

25. Quoted in Anthony Slide, *The Vaudevillians.* Westport, CT: Arlington House, 1981, p. xi.

26. Quoted in Slide, *The Vaudevillians,* p. 100.

27. Quoted in Francis Davis, *The History of the Blues.* New York: Hyperion, 1995, pp. 59–60.

28. Quoted in Smith, *America Enters the World,* p. 749.

29. Quoted in Gorton Carruth, *The Encyclopedia of American Facts and Dates,* 9th ed. New York: HarperCollins, 1993, p. 419.

30. Quoted in Matthew T. Downey et al., eds., *The Twentieth Century: The Progressive Era and the First World War.* New York: Macmillan, 1992, p. 67.

31. Quoted in Carruth, *The Encyclopedia of American Facts and Dates,* p.387.

32. Quoted in Davidson, *Life in America,* p. 182.

33. Quoted in Downey et al., *The Twentieth Century,* p. 69.

34. Quoted in Mark Sullivan, *Our Times: The United States 1900–1925,* vol. 5, *Over Here.* New York: Charles Scribner's Sons, 1933, p. 597.

Chapter Four: Edging into World Affairs

35. Quoted in Winthrop D. Jordan, Miriam Greenblatt, and John S. Bowes, *The Americans: The History of a People and a Nation.* Evanston, IL: McDougal, Littell, 1985, p. 210.

36. Quoted in Dulles, *The United States Since 1865,* p. 157.

37. Quoted in Jordan, Greenblatt, and Bowes, *The Americans,* p. 499.

38. Quoted in Jeffrey et al., *The American People,* p. 688.

39. Quoted in Jeffrey et al., *The American People,* p. 680.

40. Quoted in Bailey, *The American Pageant,* p. 678.

41. Quoted in Burns, *Workshop of Democracy,* p. 400.

42. Quoted in Garraty, *The American Nation,* p. 679.

43. Quoted in Burns, *Workshop of Democracy,* p. 410.

44. Quoted in Sullivan, *Our Times,* vol. 5, *Over Here,* p. 44.

Chapter Five: The United States Goes to War

45. Quoted in Sullivan, *Our Times: The United States 1900–1925*, vol. 4, *The War Begins*. New York: Charles Scribner's Sons, 1932, p. 41.

46. Quoted in S. L. A. Marshall, *The American Heritage History of World War I*. New York: American Heritage, 1964, p. 9.

47. Quoted in Smith, *America Enters the World*, p. 446.

48. Quoted in Sullivan, *Our Times*, vol. 5, *Over Here*, p. 59.

49. Quoted in Smith, *America Enters the World*, p. 445.

50. Quoted in Jeffrey et al., *The American People*, p. 756.

51. Quoted in Garraty, *The American Nation*, p. 697.

52. Quoted in Smith, *America Enters the World*, p. 518.

53. Quoted in Bailey, *The American Pageant*, p. 770.

54. Quoted in Ronald Schaffer, *America in the Great War: The Rise of the War Welfare State*. New York: Oxford University Press, 1991, p. 5.

55. Quoted in Burns, *Workshop of Democracy*, p. 427.

56. Quoted in Sullivan, *Our Times*, vol. 5, *Over Here*, p. 372.

57. Quoted in Edey, *This Fabulous Century*, p. 235.

58. Quoted in Smith, *America Enters the World*, p. 475.

59. Quoted in Schaffer, *America in the Great War*, p. 26.

60. Quoted in Smith, *America Enters the World*, p. 540.

61. Quoted in Schaffer, *America in the Great War*, p. 15.

62. Quoted in Smith, *America Enters the World*, p. 552.

63. Quoted in Sullivan, *Our Times*, vol. 5, *Over Here*, p. 486.

64. Quoted in Smith, *America Enters the World*, p. 482.

65. Quoted in Smith, *America Enters the World*, p. 521.

Chapter Six: The United States Helps Win the War

66. Quoted in Edey, *This Fabulous Century*, p. 208.

67. Quoted in Smith, *America Enters the World*, p. 584.

68. Quoted in Sullivan, *Our Times*, vol. 5, *Over Here*, p. 318.

69. Quoted in Schaffer, *America in the Great War*, p. 87.

70. Quoted in Florette Henri, *Bitter Victory: A History of Black Soldiers in World War I*. Garden City, NY: Doubleday, 1970, p. 83.

71. Quoted in Sullivan, *Our Times*, vol. 5, *Over Here*, p. 451.

72. Quoted in Samuel Eliot Morison, Henry Steele Commager, and William E. Leuchtenberg, *A Concise History of the American Republic*. New York: Oxford

University Press, 1977, p. 560.

73. Quoted in Uschan, *A Multicultural Portrait of World War I*, p. 67.

74. Quoted in Robert Kelley, *The Shaping of the American Past*, 4th ed., vol. 2. Englewood Cliffs, NJ: 1986, p. 532.

Chapter Seven: The Postwar Period

75. Quoted in Brooks, *Toil and Trouble*, p. 137.

76. Quoted in Sullivan, *Our Times,* vol. 5, *Over Here*, p. 531.

77. Quoted in Kelley, *The Shaping of the American Past,* p. 534.

78. Quoted in Morison, Commager, and Leuchtenberg, *A Concise History of the American Republic*, p. 563.

79. Quoted in Garraty, *The American Nation*, p. 703.

80. Quoted in Smith, *America Enters the World*, p. 775.

81. Quoted in Jordan, Greenblatt, and Bowes, *The Americans*, p. 579.

82. Quoted in Samuel Eliot Morison, *The Oxford History of the American People,* vol. 3, *1869 Through the Death of John F. Kennedy, 1963.* New York: Penguin Books USA, 1994, p. 234.

83. Quoted in John A. Garraty, ed., *The Young Reader's Companion to American History.* Boston: Houghton Mifflin, 1994, p. 417.

84. Quoted in Schaffer, *America in the Great War,* p. 89.

85. Quoted in Smith, *America Enters the World,* p. 780.

86. Quoted in Kelley, *The Shaping of the American Past*, p. 549.

Epilogue: A Mood of Pessimism

87. Quoted in Sullivan, *Our Times,* vol. 5, *Over Here,* p. 33.

88. Quoted in Davidson et al., *Nation of Nations,* p. 908.

89. Quoted in Smith, *America Enters the World,* p. 749.

90. Quoted in Smith, *America Enters the World,* p. 310.

91. Quoted in Dulles, *The United States Since 1865,* p. 274.

Chronology

1910

March 26: Congress amends the Immigration Act of 1907 to exclude paupers, criminals, anarchists, and diseased persons.

April 18: Suffragists present a petition with 500,000 names to senators and representatives supporting the right of women to vote.

June 18: Congress passes the Mann-Elkins Railroad Act giving the Interstate Commerce Commission jurisdiction over telephone, telegraphy, and cable companies.

June 24: Congress passes legislation requiring all passenger ships leaving the United States to carry radio equipment.

June 25: Congress adopts the Mann Act, which prohibits transportation of women from one state to another for prostitution, and the Publicity Act, which makes it mandatory for representatives to report campaign contributions.

November 8: Democrats win control of Congress for the first time since 1894.

November 14: A Curtiss biplane flown by Eugene Ely is the first airplane to take off from the deck of a U.S. warship, the USS *Birmingham*.

1911

February 3: The electric self-starter for automobiles is demonstrated.

March 7: President Taft orders twenty thousand soldiers to the Mexican border to protect American interests during a revolution led by Francisco Madero; they are recalled June 24.

March 25: The Triangle Shirtwaist fire kills 146 garment workers in New York City.

May 15: The Supreme Court breaks up Standard Oil Company of New Jersey, saying the giant firm is guilty of "unreasonable" restraint of trade.

May 29: The Supreme Court rules that the "tobacco trust" is in violation of the Sherman Antitrust Act.

July 24: The United States and Japan renew their commercial treaty, which includes a "gentleman's agreement" under which Japan pledges not to issue passports to laborers who want to immigrate to the United States.

September 12–November 5: Calbraith R. Rodgers flies from New York City to Long Beach, California, in a Wright biplane; the first cross-country airplane flight takes 82 hours and 4 minutes; the flying time is spread over seven weeks.

1912

January 6: New Mexico becomes the forty-seventh state.

January 9: U.S. Marines arrive in Honduras to protect American property.

January 22: U.S. troops begin occupation of Tientsin, China, to protect American interests.

February 14: Arizona becomes the forty-eighth state.

February 25: Former president Theodore Roosevelt announces his candidacy for the Republican nomination for president.

April 15: The *Titanic* sinks with the loss of 1,513 lives.

June 1: Lieutenant Henry H. Arnold of the Signal Corps sets an altitude record of 6,540 feet in a Burgess-Wright airplane.

June 5: U.S. Marines land in Cuba to protect American interests during political disorders.

June 18–22: William Howard Taft and James Sherman are nominated for president and vice president respectively, at the Republican National Convention.

June 19: Federal government extends the eight-hour day labor law to all federal workers.

June 25–July 2: New Jersey governor Woodrow Wilson is nominated for president and Thomas R. Marshall for vice president at the Democratic National Convention.

August 5–7: The Progressive Party nominates Theodore Roosevelt for president and Senator Hiram Johnson of California for vice president.

August 24: Congress makes Alaska a U.S. territory and authorizes the U.S. Post Office to deliver small parcels starting January 1, 1913.

November 5: Woodrow Wilson is elected the twenty-eighth president.

1913

January–April 21: About 150,000 garment workers strike in New York City; the strike spreads to Boston; both are settled and strikers win all demands.

February 25: The Sixteenth Amendment to the Constitution becomes law, giving Congress power to levy and collect income taxes.

March 1: Congress adopts the Webb-Kenyon Interstate Liquor Act over the veto of President Taft, making it illegal to ship liquor into states where its sale is prohibited.

May 31: The Seventeenth Amendment to the Constitution becomes law; it provides for direct election of U.S. senators.

October 3: Congress imposes the first personal income tax.

1914

April 9: U.S. Marines land at Tampico, Mexico, to take on supplies and are arrested by Mexican officials.

April 21: U.S. Marines seize Veracruz and occupy it until November 23.

May 7: Congress passes a resolution designating the second Sunday in May as Mother's Day.

June 28: Austrian archduke Franz Ferdinand and his wife, Sophie, are assassinated by a Serbian nationalist in Sarajevo, igniting World War I.

July 28: Austria-Hungary declares war on Serbia.

August 4: German infantry invades neutral Belgium, the first step in moving against France; Wilson proclaims the United States will remain neutral in the fighting that has broken out in Europe and offers to negotiate a peace settlement.

August 15: The Panama Canal opens.

September 6–10: The Battle of the Marne halts the German advance toward Paris; the end of the battle marks the beginning of trench warfare as both sides start digging in along a line that will become known as the western front.

October 4: Wilson declares this day "Peace Sunday" and asks the nation to pray for peace.

October 15: Congress passes the Clayton Antitrust Act, which reinforces and extends the Sherman Antitrust Act.

1915

January 2: Senate passes a bill requiring a literary test for immigrants; President Wilson vetoes it January 28.

January 25: Alexander Graham Bell places the first transcontinental telephone call from New York to San Francisco; Supreme Court rules Kansas may not forbid an employer to refuse employment on grounds of union membership.

January 28: Congress creates the U.S. Coast Guard.

February 8: A twelve-reel motion picture, *Birth of a Nation,* makes its debut in Los Angeles; it is hailed as a landmark in development of the movie industry.

April 5: Jess Willard knocks out Jack Johnson in the twenty-third round in Havana, Cuba, to become heavyweight champion.

May 7: A German submarine lying ten miles off the Irish coast sinks the *Lusitania,* a British passenger ship sailing from New York to Liverpool, England; nearly 1,200 people die, including 128 Americans.

May 13–June 1: The United States, in a series of diplomatic moves, protests the sinking of the *Lusitania,* and demands reparations and an end to unrestricted submarine warfare.

July 29: U.S. Marines land in Haiti after the murder of President Guillaume Sam. They remain there to protect American interests until 1936.

August 4–6: German aircraft bomb English towns marking the beginning of aerial warfare.

October 5: Germany apologizes for the *Lusitania* sinking and offers reparations.

October 15: American bankers agree to lend Great Britain and France $500 million, the largest loan in history.

October 19: The United States recognizes Venustiano Carranza as president of Mexico.

December 18: Wilson, a widower, marries Edith Bolling Galt, a widow, at her home in Washington, D.C.

1916

February 29: South Carolina passes child labor laws raising the minimum working age in mills, mines, and factories from twelve to fourteen.

March 9: Angered by U.S. recognition of Carranza, revolutionary Francisco "Pancho" Villa raids the town of Columbus, New Mexico, and a nearby camp of the 13th U.S. Cavalry; nine civilians and eight soldiers are killed; Wilson sends General John J. Pershing to capture Villa, but the mission fails.

April 18: Wilson issues an ultimatum to Germany to end unrestricted submarine warfare.

May: U.S. troops land in Santo Domingo to settle internal violence; the occupation continues until 1924.

May 4: Germany agrees not to attack ships without warning and without giving passengers a chance to escape.

June 3: Congress passes the National Defense Act which increases the 24,000-man regular army to 220,000 in five years and the National Guard to 450,000.

June 7: The Progressive Party nominates Theodore Roosevelt for president but he refuses to run and supports Chief Justice Charles Evans Hughes.

June 7–10: Hughes is nominated for president and Charles W. Fairbanks for vice president at the Republican National Convention.

June 14–16: Wilson and Marshall are renominated at the Democratic National Convention.

July 11: Wilson signs the Federal Aid Road Act, which gives states $5 million for road construction; almost 250,000 commercial vehicles and 3 million private cars are now registered to use public roads.

July 22: Ten people are killed and scores wounded when a bomb is thrown during a Preparedness Day parade in San Francisco; Thomas Mooney and others involved in the labor movement are arrested.

July 30: German saboteurs explode a munitions dump in New Jersey, causing an estimated $22 million in damages.

August 4: The United States purchases the Virgin Islands from Denmark for $25 million.

November 7: Wilson wins reelection and the Democrats take control of both Houses of Congress.

November 29: American military forces occupy the Dominican Republic after disorders in that country; the occupation does not end until October 21, 1922.

1917

January 22: Wilson tells the Senate he would like to see a "peace without victory" in World War I and suggests creation of an international group to maintain peace in the future.

January 28: Wilson orders Pershing to end his unsuccessful pursuit of Pancho Villa; Pershing withdraws from Mexico February 5.

January 31: Germany notifies the United States that unrestricted submarine warfare will resume despite the agreement reached May 4, 1916.

February 3: President Wilson suspends diplomatic relations with Germany after a German submarine sinks the USS *Housatonic.*

February 5: Congress overrides President Wilson's veto to pass an immigration act that requires a literacy test for all immigrants and bars most Asian laborers.

March 2: Passage of the Jones Act makes Puerto Rico a U.S. territory and its residents U.S. citizens.

March 5: Wilson is inaugurated for a second term.

March 16: U.S. ships *City of Memphis, Illinois,* and *Valencia* are reported sunk by submarines.

April 6: The United States declares war on Germany.

May 18: Wilson signs the bill authorizing the Selective Service Act, which creates the military draft.

June 13: Pershing, who heads the American Expeditionary Force, arrives in France with his staff; the first U.S. troops arrive two weeks later.

June 15: Congress approves the Espionage

Act, which punishes anyone who hinders the war effort or aids the enemy.

July 14: House of Representatives appropriates $640 million for a military aviation program.

July 24: The House approves spending $640 million for a fleet of airplanes.

August 10: Congress passes the Lever Food and Fuel Control Act, providing for controls on the economy during the war to maximize production and hold down waste.

October 3: Congress passes the War Revenue Act, increasing personal and corporate income taxes and establishing excise, excess profit, and luxury taxes to boost revenue needed for the war.

October 6: Congress passes the Trading with the Enemy Act, which gives the government control over foreign trade and power to censor foreign mail.

October 25: Wilson meets in the White House with one hundred members of the New York State Woman's Suffrage Party; he endorses passage of equal suffrage.

October 31: The first U.S. troops are sent to the front in France.

December 7: The United States declares war against Austria-Hungary.

December 18: The House passes the Eighteenth Amendment; one day later the Senate follows suit; ratification by the states two years later makes illegal the sale and consumption of alcoholic beverages.

1918

January 8: Wilson delivers his Fourteen Points speech, which serves as a framework for peace talks at the end of the war.

January 10: The Senate passes the Susan B.

Anthony resolution and in 1920 ratification makes it the Nineteenth Amendment to the Constitution; women voted nationally for the first time in the November 1920 presidential election.

April 8: The National War Labor Board is established to handle labor disputes; it bars strikes or lockouts but recognizes the right of workers to organize and bargain collectively.

April 20: Congress passes the Sabotage Act, directed primarily at the Industrial Workers of the World.

May 15: The first U.S. airmail service begins between New York City and Washington, D.C.

May 16: Congress approves the Sedition Act, which punishes those who interfere with the war effort.

June 3–6: U.S. troops stop the German advance at Château-Thierry and Neuilly.

June 6–July 1: U.S. troops take part in the Battle of Belleau Wood.

July 18–August 6: Second Battle of the Marne is the turning point in the war; eighty-five thousand American soldiers help stop the German offensive.

September: An epidemic of influenza, which originated in Europe, hits the United States; before it is over in 1919 the outbreak of flu kills five hundred thousand Americans, many of them soldiers in military camps overseas.

November 5: In midterm elections Republicans take control of both the House and Senate.

November 9: German kaiser Wilhelm II abdicates and flees Germany.

November 11: Armistice Day, the end of

World War I, celebrated as an annual holiday for the first time one year later.

1919

January 18: Wilson attends the opening session of peace talks in Paris.

January 25–February 14: The covenant of the proposed League of Nations is drafted.

January 29: The Eighteenth Amendment to the Constitution is ratified, prohibiting the sale and manufacture of liquor in the United States.

May 21: A Curtiss NC-4 seaplane that took off from Rockaway, New York, reaches England via Newfoundland, the Azores, and Portugal in the first air crossing of the Atlantic Ocean; the flight takes eighteen days.

June 28: The Treaty of Versailles is signed by Wilson and other heads of state at Versailles, France.

September 22: More than 360,000 workers strike against the U.S. Steel Corporation and other companies that still require a twelve-hour workday; the strike is broken by military force four months later.

September 25: Wilson suffers a stroke in Pueblo, Colorado, while on a tour to build support for the Versailles treaty, limiting his ability to govern for the rest of his term.

October 28: The Volstead Act, which provides enforcement for the eighteenth Amendment, is passed over Wilson's veto; it goes into effect January 16, 1920, making America a "dry" nation.

December 22: A series of raids is organized by Attorney General A. Mitchell Palmer to round up suspected Communists following a wave of anticommunist hysteria; the raids are carried out from January through May of 1920.

For Further Reading

Peter I. Bosco, *World War I: America at War.* New York: Facts On File, 1991.

Maitland A. Edey, ed., *This Fabulous Century.* Vol. 2, *1910–1920.* New York: Time-Life Books, 1969.

John A. Garraty, ed., *The Young Reader's Companion to American History.* Boston: Houghton Mifflin, 1994.

Ernest R. May, *A Proud Nation.* Evanston, IL.: McDougall, Littell, 1985.

George R. Metcalf, *Black Profiles.* New York: McGraw-Hill, 1970.

George Sullivan, *The Day the Women Got the Vote.* New York: Scholastic, 1994.

Michael V. Uschan, *A Multicultural Portrait of World War I.* New York: Marshall Cavendish, 1996.

Works Consulted

Thomas A. Bailey, *The American Pageant*. 5th ed., vol. 2. Lexington, MA: D. C. Heath, 1975.

John Baxter, *Sixty Years of Hollywood*. New York: A. S. Barnes, 1973.

Thomas R. Brooks, *Toil and Trouble: A History of American Labor,* 2nd ed. New York: Delacorte, 1971.

James MacGregor Burns, *Workshop of Democracy: The American Experiment*. Vol. 2. New York: Knopf, 1985.

Gorton Carruth, *The Encyclopedia of American Facts and Dates*. 9th ed. New York: HarperCollins, 1993.

John Clements, *Chronology of the United States*. New York: McGraw-Hill, 1975.

James West Davidson et al., *Nation of Nations: A Narrative History of the American Republic*. New York: McGraw-Hill, 1994.

Marshall B. Davidson, *Life in America*. Vol. 2. Boston: Houghton Mifflin, 1951.

Francis Davis, *The History of the Blues*. New York: Hyperion, 1995.

Matthew T. Downey et al., eds., *The Twentieth Century: The Progressive Era and the First World War*. New York: Macmillan, 1992.

Phillip T. Drotning, *Black Heroes in Our Nation's History*. New York: Cowles, 1869.

Foster Rhea Dulles, *The United States Since 1865*. Ann Arbor: University of Michigan Press, 1971.

Jerry Epstein, *Remembering Charlie: A Pictorial Biography*. New York: Doubleday, 1989.

Sara M. Evans, *Born for Liberty: A History of Women in America*. New York: Macmillan, 1989.

John A. Garraty, *The American Nation*. Vol. 2, *A History of the United States Since 1865*. New York: HarperCollins, 1991.

————, *Woodrow Wilson*. New York: Knopf, 1956.

Lettie Gavin, *American Women in World War I*. Niwot: University Press of Colorado, 1997.

Eli Ginzberg and Hyman Berman, *The American Worker in the Twentieth Century*. New York: Free Press of Glencoe, 1963.

Florette Henri. *Bitter Victory: A History of Black Soldiers in World War I*. Garden City, NY: Doubleday, 1970.

Julie Roy Jeffrey et al., eds., *The American People: Creating a Nation and a Society*. 2nd ed. New York: HarperCollins, 1990.

Winthrop D. Jordan, Miriam Greenblatt, and John S. Bowes, *The Americans: The History of a People and a Nation*. Evanston, IL: McDougal, Littell, 1985.

Robert Kelley, *The Shaping of the American Past*. 4th ed., vol. 2. Englewood Cliffs, NJ: 1986.

Don Lawson, *The United States in World War I*. New York: Alfred-Schuman, 1963.

Calvin D. Linton, ed., *The Bicentennial Almanac*. Nashville: Thomas Nelson, 1975.

Arthur Little, *From Harlem to the Rhine*. New York: Covici Friede, 1936.

S. L. A. Marshall, *The American Heritage History of World War I*. New York: American Heritage, 1964.

Ernest R. May, *The Life History of the United States.* Vol. 9, *1901–1917.* New York: Time-Life Books, 1974.

Samuel Eliot Morison,*The Oxford History of the American People.* Vol. 3, *1869 Through the Death of John F. Kennedy, 1963.* New York: Penguin Books USA, 1994.

Samuel Eliot Morison, Henry Steele Commager, and William E. Leuchtenberg, *A Concise History of the American Republic.* New York: Oxford University Press, 1977.

Ronald Schaffer, *America in the Great War: The Rise of the War Welfare State.* New York: Oxford University Press, 1991.

Upton Sinclair, *The Jungle.* New York: Bantam Books, 1981.

Anthony Slide, *The Vaudevillians.* Westport, CT: Arlington House, 1981.

Page Smith, *America Enters the World: A People's History of the Progressive Era and World War I.* New York: McGraw-Hill, 1985.

Ray Stuart, *Immortals of the Screen.* New York: Bonanza Books, 1965.

Mark Sullivan, *Our Times: The United States 1900–1925.* Vol. 4, *The War Begins.* New York: Charles Scribner's Sons, 1932.

————, *Our Times: The United States 1900–1925.* Vol. 5, *Over Here.* New York: Charles Scribner's Sons, 1933.

Index

actors, 38–39
Adamson Act, 19
Addams, Jane, 28, 29, 63–64
African Americans, 22–23, 30–32
    during postwar, 100–101
    influence on music by, 41–42
    migration of, 35, 75–77
    in the military, 84, 87
    in sports, 44, 45
airplane, 48
Alexander, Grover Cleveland, 44
Allen, Fred, 39
Allen, Gracie, 41
Allies, 61
    close defeat of, 79–80
    defeat by, 88
    and the Treaty of
        Versailles, 90
    see also France; Great Britain;
        Russia; United States
American Expeditionary Force
    (AEF), 70–71, 82
American Federation of Labor
    (AFL), 19, 23
    on capitalism, 23–24
    during wartime, 75
    membership of, 98
American Neutrality Conference
    Committee, 64
Americans
    attitude toward WW I, 63–64
    postwar mood of, 73–74,
        78, 92–93, 107–108
American Union Against
    Militarism, 64
anarchism, 27
Anderson, Sherwood, 46
Anthony, Susan B., 102
Anti-Saloon League, 103
Arbuckle, Roscoe, 38–39
Argentina, 57
Armenia, 90
Armour, Philip D., 10

Army Air Service, 86
Army Nurse Corps, 83
Army Signal Corps, 83
Asians, 28
Austria, 62, 90
Austro-Hungarian Empire, 61,
    62, 81, 88
automobile, 46–48

Babe Ruth. See Ruth, George
    Herman
Baker, Newton D., 70, 71
Balloon Buster, 86
banks, 10
    regulation of, 18–19
Bara, Theda, 39
Baruch, Bernard, 71
Battle of the Marne, 80
Belgium, 61, 62
Bell, Alexander Graham, 48–49
Benet, Rosemary, 15
Benet, Stephen Vincent, 15
Berger, Victor, 74, 75
Berle, Milton, 41
Berlin, Irving, 41
big businesses, 9–10
    efforts to regulate, 16
    postwar, 96
Big Four, 89–90
Birmingham, The, 48
blues music, 41–42
Bolshevik Revolution, 79
bonds, 72
books, 44, 46
Borah, William, 93
Bosnia, 61, 62
Bow, Clara, 39
boxing, 44, 45
Boy Scouts, 49
Brandeis, Louis D., 19, 92
Brazil, 57
Brice, Fanny, 41
Bulgaria, 61

Bullard, Robert L., 87
Burleson, Albert S., 31
Burns, George, 41
Burns, Tommy, 45

Campfire Girls, 49
Cantor, Eddie, 41
capitalism, 12, 24
    vs. socialism, 26
Carranza, Venustiano, 57–58
Carroll, Earl, 86
Cather, Willa, 44, 46
Catt, Chapman Carrie, 102, 103
Central Powers, 61
    see also Germany
Chaplin, Charlie, 36, 38–39, 40
Chicago Defender, 76
child labor, 5, 11
Chile, 57
China, 53–54, 61
Chinese Exclusion Act of 1882, 28
cities
    immigrants in, 27, 28–29
    problems in, 6–7
Citizens Military Training Corps,
    66
City of Memphis, 67
civil service, 13
Clayton Antitrust Act, 19
Clemenceau, Georges, 89
Cleveland, Grover, 10, 53
Cobb, Ty, 43–44
Cohan, George M., 41
Collier's, 12
Colombia, 55
comic strips, 44
Commission on Industrial
    Relations, 30
Committee on Public Information
    (CPI), 68–69, 88
communism, 26, 27
    during postwar, 93, 98
    see also Red Scare

conservation, 14
Coolidge, Calvin, 97
Cox, James M., 106
Creel, George, 11, 68–69, 88
Crisis, 32, 100
crossword puzzle, 44
Cuba, 52, 54, 56
currency, 19
Czechoslovakia, 62, 90

Dawson, Joe, 43
Debs, Eugene V., 14, 74, 75
Dempsey, Jack, 44
Díaz, Porfirio, 57
Dixon, Thomas, 38
Dodge, Horace, 71
dogfights, 86
Dole, Sanford B., 53
Dominican Republic, 54, 57
doughboys, 82–83
draft, 69–70, 82, 83
Dreiser, Theodore, 44, 46
Du Bois, W. E. B., 32, 33, 100
Durante, Jimmy, 41
Duryea, Charles, 46
Duryea, Frank, 46

economy, 5
   during wartime, 71–72, 75
   postwar, 96
Edison, Thomas Alva, 37
Egypt, 90
Eighteenth Amendment, 103
elections
   first primary, 13
   1912, 14–16
   1916, 19–20
Ely, Eugene, 48
Engels, Friedrich, 26
England, 82, 90
Erector Set, 49
Espionage Act, 74, 75
Estonia, 90

Fairbanks, Douglas, 39, 72
Fair Deal, 108
farming, 4, 5
Farm Loan Act, 19

Federal Child Labor Law, 19
Federal Reserve Bank, 18–19
Federal Reserve Board, 19
Federal Trade Commission, 19
Ferdinand, Archduke Franz, 61
Ferdinand, Sophie, 61
Finland, 90
fires, 21–22
First Amendment
   suppression of, 74–75
First Battle of Ypres, 81
Folk, Joseph W., 13
Food Administration, 71–72
Ford, Henry, 26, 47–48, 71
Four Minute Men, 69
Fourteen Points, 87–88
France, 61, 62, 90
   and Africa, 82
   aid from U.S. to, 85
   as member of League of
      Nations, 90
French Flying Corps, 86
Frost, Robert, 46
Fuel Administration, 71

Garros, Roland, 86
Germany, 54
   and Africa, 82
   begin WW I, 62
   request for peace to, 88
   and roots of WW I, 61
   submarine warfare by, 65–66,
      79–80
   U.S. peace treaty with, 90, 94
   and U.S. relations, 67
   war damages paid by, 89–90
Gompers, Samuel L., 27, 97
   head of AFL, 19, 23
Gould, Jay, 30
government
   effect of big business on, 10
   reform on local level, 12–14
   role of, 12, 108–109
Grayson, Cary, 94, 95
Great Britain, 54, 61, 62
   block European ports, 64
   as member of League of
      Nations, 90

in WW I, 61, 62
Great Society, 108
Great War. *See* World War I
Grey, Zane, 46
Griffith, D. W., 38
Guam, 52
Guatemala, 54

Haiti, 57
Hall of Mirrors, 90
Handy, W. C., 41–42
Harding, Warren G., 106
Hart, William S., 38
Hawaii, 52–53
Hay, W. H., 87
Haywood, William, 23–24, 75
Hello Girls, 83
Henry, Vida, 84
History of the American People, A,
   28
Hitler, Adolf, 109
Ho Chi Minh, 90
Honduras, 54
Hoover, Herbert, 71–72
Houdini, Harry, 39–40
House, Edward M., 60–61
housing. *See* tenement housing
Huerta, Victoriano, 57
Hughes, Charles Evans, 13, 67
Hughes, Evans, 19–20
Hull House, 28, 29
Hungary, 62, 90
Hunter, Robert, 5–6

Illinois, 67
immigrants
   discrimination against, 73–74
   during WW I, 63
   efforts to restrict, 98–100
   and labor surplus, 29
   and prohibition, 103–104
   rejection of, 22, 27–28
   settlement in cities by, 6–7
imperialism, 51–52
   Wilson's attempt to end, 88
income tax, 13, 18, 72
Indianapolis 500, 44
Industrial Revolution, 5–6

effect on labor by, 23
Industrial Workers of the World
    (IWW), 23–25
    opposition to war, 74, 75
industry, 71
inflation, 107
International Congress of
    Women, 63
Interstate Commerce
    Commission, 14
IPM Studio, 38
isolationism, 50–51
Italy, 61, 90

Japan, 54, 61, 90
jazz, 42
Jeffries, Jim, 45
Jews, 19
Jim Crow laws, 31, 77
Johnson, Jack, 44, 45
Johnson, Lyndon B., 108
Jones, Mary Harris "Mother", 11,
    24
Joplin, Scott, 41

Kalakaua (king of Hawaii), 53
kinetoscope, 37
Kipling, Rudyard, 51
Knights of Labor, 24
Korea, 54
Ku Klux Klan, 93

labor, 4
    African Americans in, 30–31
    child, 5, 11
    during wartime, 75–78
    effect of Industrial Revolution
        on , 5
    effect of WW I on, 35
    postwar problems of, 96–98
    women in, 77–78
    see also labor reform; labor
        unions
labor reform, 19, 22, 30
    and Henry Ford, 26
labor unions, 19, 23–25
    conflict with management,
        29–30

radicals in, 96–97
salaries under, 30
Ladies Home Journal, 12
Lafayette Escadrille, 63, 86
laissez-faire, 12
Latvia, 90
Lazarus, Emma, 100
League of Nations, 88, 89, 90–91
    criticism of, 93
    defeat of, 108, 109
    and WW II, 109
League of Women Voters, 103
League to Limit Armaments, 64
legislation
    on drinking, 104–105
    on taxes, 18
    on voting, 13, 103
Life, 64
Liliuokalani (queen of Hawaii),
    52–53
Lincoln Logs, 49
Lindsay, Vachel, 46
Lithuania, 90
Lloyd, David, 89
Lodge, Henry Cabot, 93
Loftus, Johnny, 44
London, Jack, 44, 46
Luke, Frank, Jr., 86
Lusitania, 65, 66

Madero, Francisco, 57
magazines, 46
Malawi, 82
Manchuria, 54
Marconi, Guglielmo, 49
Martin, Edward S., 64
Marx Brothers, 41
Marx, Karl, 26
Marxist socialism, 26
McClure's, 12, 74
McKinley, William, 14, 52
Messenger, 74
Methodist Church, 103
middle class, 8–9
military
    in Latin America, 55, 57
    in Mexico, 58–59
    preparations for war, 66–67,

69–70
    racism in, 84
    role of pilots/airplanes in, 86
    see also soldiers
Milwaukee Leader, 74
miners, 24, 98
Mitchell, William, 86
Mix, Tom, 38
Model T, 47, 48
Money Trust, 19
Monroe Doctrine, 54
Morgan, J. Pierpont, 10
Morrison, William, 46
Morse code, 49
Mother Jones, 11, 24
Mother's Day, 49
motion pictures. See movies
movies, 36–37
    birth of, 37–38
    prowar, 69
    stars of, 38–39
movie studios, 38
muckrakers, 12
music, 37, 41–42

National American Woman
    Suffrage Association (NAWSA),
    32–33, 34, 102, 103
National Association for the
    Advancement of Colored People
    (NAACP), 31, 32, 33, 101
National Guard, 97
National Progressive Party, 16
National War Labor Board, 71, 75
National Woman Suffrage
    Association, 102
New Deal, 108
New Freedom, 16, 108
New Nationalism, 16, 108
newspapers, 44
New York Herald, 38
New York Sunday World, The, 44
Nicaragua, 54, 56
Nicholas II (czar of Russia), 85
nickelodeons, 37–38
Nineteenth Amendment, 103
Nobel Peace Prize, 29, 54
Noble Order of the Knights of

Labor, 23

Olympic Games, 43
Orlando, Vittorio, 89
Ottoman Empire, 61, 88, 90

pacifism, 63–64, 76
Palestine, 90
Palmer, A. Mitchell, 98
Panama, 55–56
Panama Canal, 54–55
Peace Sunday, 59
Pershing, John, 59, 86
Philippine Islands, 52
Pickford, Mary, 36–37, 39
Picture Play, 39
pilots, 86
Poland, 88, 90
policemen, 97
population, 4
  in cities, 7
  of European descent, 63
Poverty, 5–6
Praeger, Robert, 73
prejudice, 27
  see also racism
Princip, Gavrilo, 61
Progressive movement, 7, 8–9
  and big business, 9–10
  and capitalism, 26
  end of, 20
  local government reform under,
    12–14
  and 1912 elections, 14
  philosophy of, 10, 12
  problems ignored by, 22–23
  under Woodrow Wilson, 16–20
  on women's movement, 33–34
prohibition, 103–104
propaganda, 68–69, 88
Puerto Rico, 52

racism, 31, 33
  in the military, 84, 87
  in movies, 38
  and violence, 101
radio, 49
ragtime music, 41

railroads, 10
Rankin, Jeannette, 76
reading, 44, 46
Red Baron, 86
Red Scare, 96–97
Reed, James, 69
Richthofen, Manfred von, 86
Rickenbacker, Eddie, 86
riots, 101
Roberts, Kenneth, 99
Robinson, Bill, 41
Rockefeller, John D., 10
Rodgers, Calbraith R., 48
Rogers, Will, 41
Roosevelt, Franklin D., 108
Roosevelt, Quentin, 86
Roosevelt, Theodore, 7, 12, 82
  foreign policy, 54–56
  in Progressive movement,
    14–16
  votes for, 16
  on women's movement, 33–34
Russia, 54
  seek peace with Germany, 85
  in WW I, 61, 62, 79, 81
Ruth, George Herman, 44

Sandburg, Carl, 46
Sarajevo, 61
Schwieger, Karl, 66
Sedition Act, 74
segregation, 31–32
Selective Service System, 69–70
Sennet, Mack, 40
Serbia, 62, 81
settlement house movement, 28–29
Seventeenth Amendment, 13
Sherman Antitrust Act, 19
silent movies. *See* movies
Sims, William S., 80
Sixteenth Amendment, 18
Socialists, 25–27
  labor union formed by, 23
  opposition to war, 74
soldiers
  arrival in France, 84–86
  deaths of/wounded, 88–90
  living conditions of, 81

training for, 82–83
  varying backgrounds of, 83–84
songs, 41
Souls of Black Folk, The, 32
Spanish-American War, 52
sports, 42–44, 45
Square Deal, 16
Standard Oil Company, 10
Stanton, Charles E., 84, 85
Stanton, Elizabeth Cady, 102
Starr, Ellen Gates, 29
Statue of Liberty, 99–100
steel, 5, 10
steelworkers, 96–97
Steffens, Lincoln, 12, 107
Stevens, John L., 53
Stimson, Julia C., 83
strikes, 24, 93, 96–98
  in textile mills, 30
Strong, Josiah, 51–52
submarine warfare, 65–66, 67,
  79–80
Sullivan, Mark, 106
Sussex, 66
Sussex Pledge, 66, 67

Taft, William Howard, 14–15, 30
  foreign policy of, 56
  votes for, 16
Tarbell, Ida, 12
tariffs, 15, 17–18
technology, 48–49
telephones, 48–49
tenement housing, 28
textile mills, 11, 30
Thorpe, Jim, 43
Tifton Gazette, 77
Titanic, 49
toys, 49
Treaty of Versailles, 89–90
  rejection of, 94
trenches, 80–81
Triangle Shirtwaist Company,
  21–22
Truman, Harry, 108
trusts, 5, 9–10
  efforts to break up, 14
  regulation of, 14–15, 19

Tulsa World, 75
Turkey, 61
Tuskegee Institute, 31
Twenty-first Amendment,
  104–105

U-boats, 65, 66
Underwood Tariff Act, 18
unemployment, 93, 107
unions. *See* labor unions
United Mine Workers, 24
United Nations, 88
United States
  annexes Hawaii, 52, 53
  attacked by German
    submarines, 65–66
  and decision to enter war,
    67–68
  effect of WW I on, 34–35, 74–78
  foreign trade by, 53–54
  help fund WW I, 72, 80
  help win WW I, 84–89
  imperialism of, 52
  intervention in Mexico, 57–59
  living conditions in, 5–6, 7
  as member of League of
    Nations, 90, 94
  preparation for WW I
    involvement, 68–69
  role in world affairs, 50–51
  trade with Allies, 65
  see also Americans
United States Steel Corporation,
  10
urbanization, 4–5
U.S. Marines, 57
U.S. Navy, 49

Vail, Theodore, 49
vaudeville, 39–41
Venezuela, 54

Veracruz, 57
Victrolas, 41
Vigilancia, 67
Villa, Francisco "Pancho", 58–59
Villard, Oswald Garrison, 78
Virgin Islands, 57
Volstead Act, 103
voting
  by African Americans, 32, 101
  by women, 32–34, 101–103

Walsh, Frank, 30
War Industries Board, 71
Washington, Booker T., 31–32
Waters, Ethel, 41
Watson, Thomas A., 48–49
White, William Allen, 15, 65
White House, 38
Wilcox, Howard, 44
Wilhelm II, Kaiser, 88
Willard, Jess, 44, 45
Williams, Eugene, 101
Wilson, Edith, 94
Wilson, Woodrow, 7, 13–14
  on African Americans, 30–31
  argues for peace, 87–88
  criticism of, 93
  declares a strike, 98
  declares war, 67
  defeat/illness of, 94, 95
  foreign policy of, 57–58
  on immigrants, 27–28,
    98–100
  and the League of Nations, 91
  legacy of, 106, 108–109
  participation in peace talks by,
    89–90
  preparation for war under,
    66–67, 68, 69–70
  reform under, 16–20
  on submarine warfare, 65–66

on women's movement, 34
on WW I, 59, 60–61, 64
Wisconsin Idea, 13
women
  first in Congress, 76
  in the labor force, 77–78
  voting by, 32–34, 101–103
  in WW I, 83
Women's Army Motor Corps,
  83
Women's Christian Temperance
  Union, 103
Women's International League for
  Peace and Freedom, 29
Women's Peace Party, 63, 64
women's suffrage, 32–34,
  101–103
World Series, 42–43
World War I, 20, 80–81
  casualties, 81, 88–89
  change in labor force during,
    75–78
  control of economy during,
    71–72
  cost of, 72
  effect of, 34–35, 107–108
  as global war, 81–82
  outbreak of, 59
  roots of, 61–63
  see also submarine warfare
World War II, 109
Wright, John L., 49
Wright brothers, 48
Wynn, Ed, 41
Wynne, Arthur, 44

Yale Bowl, 44
Yugoslavia, 90

zeppelins, 86
Zimmerman, Arthur, 67

Picture Credits

About the Author

Michael V. Uschan has written five books including *A Multicultural Portrait of World War I*, *A Basic Guide to Luge*, part of a series written for the U.S. Olympic Committee, and a book in this series on the 1940s. Mr. Uschan began his career as a writer and editor with United Press International, a wire service that provides news reports to newspapers, radio, and television. Because journalism is sometimes called "history in a hurry," he considers writing history books a natural extension of the skills he developed as a journalist. He and his wife, Barbara, live in Franklin, Wisconsin, a suburb of Milwaukee.

DATE DUE